FOUR MINUTES AND SEVENTEEN SECONDS

How One Conversation Changes Everything in a **Dental Practice**

Tammy Duncan

Copyright & Disclaimer

Four Minutes and Seventeen Seconds: How One Conversation Changes Everything in a Dental Practice

Library of Congress Control Number: 2026914449

Disclaimer

The content of this book is intended for professional development and educational purposes only. The strategies, language examples, communication frameworks, and practice management principles contained herein are provided as general guidance and do not constitute legal, clinical, financial, regulatory, or compliance advice of any kind.

Results described or implied throughout this book are not guaranteed. Individual outcomes will vary based on practice size, market, team composition, patient demographics, implementation consistency, and other factors outside the control of the author or Practice Management Systems®.

The author has made every effort to ensure the accuracy and completeness of the information presented. However, neither the author nor Practice Management Systems® assumes any liability for errors, omissions, or outcomes resulting from the use or application of any material contained in this publication.

Not perfectly. Not all at once. Not with the anxiety of someone who feels the weight of sixteen chapters pressing down on the first Monday morning of the implementation.

One week at a time. One focus at a time. One specific language change practiced consistently until it becomes automatic — and then the next one.

Start this week. Not next month when things settle down. Not after the next team meeting. This week.

Pick one thing from the 90-day plan — the phone audit, the Team Language Inventory, the conversation with the dentist about buy-in. Pick the one that feels most immediately possible and do it before Friday.

Because the practice that starts imperfectly this week will always outperform the practice that waits for the perfect moment that never quite arrives.

The next word your team speaks is the beginning. Make it the right one.

Conclusion — The conversation that started everything. And the one that starts yours.

Real-world scenarios and composite examples used throughout this book are drawn from general professional experience and are intended to illustrate communication principles only. Any resemblance to specific individuals, practices, or situations is coincidental unless explicitly stated.

The author's credentials, certifications, and professional affiliations referenced in this book were accurate at the time of publication. Readers are encouraged to verify current information at www.practice-sys.com.

First Edition — 2026 Printed in the United States of America

Practice Management Systems® www.practice-sys.com Oregon, United States

Dedication

For David. You always knew — even when I didn't. You are the reason I kept going on every day I wanted to stop.

For Amanda — your strength, your grace, and the way you love take my breath away. You became someone I look up to long before you knew I was watching. And for Riley and Brody — you are proof that the best things we ever build are the ones that outlast us. Watch this world — it needs everything you are bringing to it.

For Alyssa — your light fills every room you walk into and every heart you touch. You have always known how to make hard things feel like they were never hard at all. And for Sadie, Allie, and Tatum — three souls so full of joy that being in the same room with you makes everything else make sense. You are my favorite reason to build something lasting.

Contents

FORWARD

While Tammy is my mom, our relationship extends far beyond that. For more than 14 years, we've worked side by side in the dental industry. Technically, she was never my boss—she didn't sign my paychecks—but while I managed multiple dental practices she consulted with, she was absolutely the person I looked to for guidance.

No matter the challenge—a difficult patient conversation, a team conflict, a scheduling crisis, or an insurance headache—Tammy was my first call. Time and time again, she brought clarity, wisdom, and practical solutions. She has a unique ability to see what others missed and a gift for helping people navigate even the most complicated situations with confidence.

In fact, there was one thing I heard over and over again from dentists, office managers, and team members who worked with her:

"I wish I could keep Tammy in my pocket."

This book is the closest thing to that.

What makes Tammy so effective is that she has never taught from the sidelines. She has spent decades in the trenches of dentistry—as a dental assistant, treatment coordinator, scheduler, office manager, consultant, and coach. She understands the realities of a dental practice because she has lived them. The principles, systems, and insights in these pages weren't developed in theory; they were refined through years of hands-on experience helping practices overcome challenges and thrive.

For more than 20 years, Tammy has dedicated herself to helping dental teams succeed by transferring the knowledge, instincts, and heart for people that come so naturally to her. She has poured herself into coaching practices, developing leaders, improving patient experiences, and creating stronger, healthier teams. This book is the culmination of that work. It captures the lessons she's spent a lifetime learning and places them into the hands of dental professionals everywhere.

What excites me most is imagining the ripple effect this book will create.

As dentists and team members embrace these principles, they'll experience greater confidence, stronger teams, smoother days, and renewed joy in the work they do. But the impact won't stop there.

Every day, patients walk into dental offices carrying fear, anxiety, embarrassment, or uncertainty. The way a practice communicates, serves, and cares for them can change their entire experience—not only with dentistry, but with their health. My hope is that the wisdom in these pages helps transform those experiences, replacing fear with trust, confusion with understanding, and hesitation with hope.

This book is more than a guide for building a successful dental practice. It's an invitation to create better experiences for patients, stronger cultures for teams, and a greater sense of purpose in the work we do every day.

I can't think of a better person to place that wisdom into your hands than Tammy.

So if you've ever wished you had an experienced mentor sitting beside you, guiding you through the challenges of practice management, patient care, and team leadership, you're in luck.

Alyssa Williams
Former Dental Practice Manager
Leadership Coach
Proud Daughter and Lifelong Student of Tammy Duncan's Wisdom

How to Use This Book

This book was written to be used — not just read.

It was not written to sit on a shelf and look impressive. It was not written to be skimmed on a flight and forgotten by the time the wheels touch down. It was written to be underlined, dog-eared, argued with, shared with your team, and returned to again and again as your practice grows and the conversations you have every day get better and better.

Here is how to get the most out of it.

Read it once all the way through — first.

Resist the temptation to jump to the chapter that feels most urgent. The book is structured deliberately — each section builds on the one before it. Part One establishes why the problem exists. Part Two gives you the framework to address it. Part Three shows you what that framework looks like in every specific conversation your practice has. Part Four shows you what your practice looks like when it all comes together — and gives you the exact plan to get there.

Read it in order the first time. Then go back to the chapters that matter most for where you are right now.

Read it with someone.

This book is most powerful when it is not read alone. Share it with your office manager. Read it alongside your team. Use the chapter takeaways as the starting point for a team conversation about what needs to change and what is already working.

The practices that transform fastest are not the ones where one person read a book and tried to implement it alone. They are the ones where the whole team encountered the ideas together and decided together to do something different.

Read it as a mirror — not a manual.

Every chapter in this book describes something real that is happening in dental practices everywhere. Some of it will be uncomfortable to recognize. Some of it will make you wince at a phrase you said just last Tuesday. Some of it will make you want to call your front desk coordinator and say — we need to talk.

That discomfort is not a problem. It is the point. Awareness — the first pillar of A.L.I.G.N.™ — begins with the willingness to see clearly. Let this book show you what is there. Then use the rest of it to change what needs changing.

Use Chapter 16 as your action plan.

The 90-Day A.L.I.G.N.™ Implementation Plan in Chapter 16 is not an appendix. It is the bridge between reading this book and living it. When you finish the final chapter go directly to Chapter 16 and begin building your specific week-by-week plan before the inspiration fades and the Monday morning schedule takes over.

The practices that change are the ones that start before they feel completely ready. Start before you feel completely ready.

Keep it close.

The best thing that can happen to this book is that it gets worn out. That the spine cracks from being opened too many times. That the margins fill up with notes. That the pages get coffee-stained from being read at the front desk between patients.

A pristine book on a shelf helped nobody.

A worn-out book in the hands of a team that communicates differently because of it — that is the whole point.

One final note before you begin:

This book is going to ask something of you. It is going to ask you to look honestly at how your practice communicates — and to sit with what you find long enough to actually change it. That is not always comfortable. But it is always worth it.

The practices described in these pages — the ones that make patients feel genuinely cared for, that retain their teams, that grow because they serve exceptionally well — are not exceptional because they found better technology or bigger marketing budgets or more aggressive production targets.

They are exceptional because someone decided that the words mattered.

You are holding the proof that they do.

Now — let us begin.

A quick guide to the book's structure:

Introduction — The most expensive sentence in dentistry and why this book exists.

Part One — The Problem — Why communication gaps are costing dental practices more than anyone realizes — and why the team is never the problem.

Part Two — The Framework — The complete A.L.I.G.N.™ system — Awareness, Language, Identity, Goals, and Navigation — explained in depth across five dedicated chapters.

Part Three — Putting It Into Practice — The A.L.I.G.N.™ framework applied to every specific communication category in the dental practice — new patients, scheduling, insurance, financial conversations, treatment acceptance, hygiene, reactivation, front office, and team leadership.

Part Four — The Transformation — What a fully aligned practice looks and feels like — and the specific 90-day plan to become one.

What This Means for Your Practice

We have arrived at the chapter that everything before it was building toward.

Not because the previous fifteen chapters were preparation for the real work. They were the real work. The awareness you developed. The language you examined. The identity questions you sat with honestly. The goals you set specifically. The navigation systems you began to understand.

All of it matters. All of it is essential. And all of it now needs one more thing to become genuinely transformative rather than genuinely interesting.

It needs to be implemented.

Chapter 1

The Words Are Costing You

"People may hear your words, but they feel your attitude." — John Maxwell

Picture this.

It is a Tuesday morning. The phones are ringing, the schedule is full, and somewhere in the back of the practice a hygienist is setting up for her first patient. The front desk coordinator — let's call her Michelle — is doing three things at once. She is checking in a patient, responding to an email, and watching the hold light blink on line two.

She picks up line two.

A woman's voice — warm, a little hesitant. She is calling for the first time. She found the practice online, read a few reviews, liked what she saw. She has not been to the dentist in two years and she is already a little nervous about making this call at all. But she is trying. She is reaching out. And her first question — the most natural question in the world — is this:

"Hi, I was just wondering — how much is a cleaning and exam?"

Michelle, busy and efficient and well-meaning, answers without thinking:

"We can't give fees over the phone."

Click. Not literally. The woman doesn't hang up in anger. She just gets a little quieter. A little more distant. The small amount of courage it took her to make that call deflates like a slow leak in a tire. The conversation limps forward for another thirty seconds and ends without an appointment being scheduled.

Michelle moves on to the next thing. She has no idea anything went wrong.

The woman calls the practice down the street.

That scenario is not dramatic. It is not unusual. It is happening in dental practices everywhere, every single day, dozens of times a day — and the cumulative cost of it is staggering.

Let's put some numbers around it.

The average new patient is worth somewhere between $1,500 and $3,000 to a dental practice in the first year alone — and significantly more over a lifetime of care. When you factor in treatment acceptance, hygiene recare, and referrals from a happy patient, a single new patient relationship can be worth $10,000 or more to a practice over five to ten years.

Now think about Michelle's Tuesday morning. If that exchange — those eight words, "we can't give fees over the phone" — costs the practice one potential new patient per day, five days a week, fifty weeks a year — the math becomes impossible to ignore.

One lost new patient per day. At a conservative $1,500 lifetime value.

That is $375,000 a year.

Walking out the door. Before the patient ever walked in.

And Michelle had no idea.

"The single biggest problem in communication is the illusion that it has taken place." — often attributed to George Bernard Shaw, frequently cited by John Maxwell

Here is the hard truth that most practice management conversations avoid:

The problem is almost never the dentistry.

In over 38 years of working inside dental practices — sitting at the front desk, standing in the hallway, listening to phone calls, watching financial conversations unfold in real time — I have rarely walked into a practice and found a clinical problem at the root of the practice's struggles. The dentists I work with are skilled. Many of them are exceptional. They went to school for nearly a decade. They invest in continuing education. They genuinely care about their patients' health.

But caring about your patients' health and communicating that care effectively are two entirely different skill sets — and dental school teaches exactly one of them.

The result is a profession full of gifted clinicians leading teams that are linguistically unprepared for the most important conversations they have every single day.

Not because they are bad at their jobs. Not because they don't care. But because nobody ever taught them that the words matter as much as the work.

The Gap Nobody Talks About

There is a gap in most dental practices between what the team thinks they are communicating and what the patient actually hears.

It is not a gap of intention. Everyone in the practice wants the patient to feel welcome, cared for, and confident. The gap is one of awareness — the team simply does not know what their words are doing on the other end of the conversation.

Consider these common exchanges and what they actually communicate to the patient hearing them:

When a team member says *"We're booked"* — the patient hears: *"You are not a priority."*

When a team member says *"Your insurance doesn't cover that"* — the patient hears: *"You're on your own."*

When a team member says *"You need to floss more"* — the patient hears: *"You're doing it wrong and it's your fault."*

When a team member says *"Are you still coming tomorrow?"* — the patient hears: *"We're expecting you to cancel."*

None of these are what the team member meant. But meaning and impact are not the same thing. As John Maxwell puts it:

"Communication is not just about what you say. It's about what the other person receives."

And what patients receive — moment by moment, call by call, appointment by appointment — determines whether they trust you, whether they return, whether they accept treatment, and whether they tell others about you. Every single word is either building that trust or quietly eroding it.

The Compounding Cost of Careless Language

The financial cost of poor communication in a dental practice is not just about lost new patients. It compounds across every category of practice performance.

Case acceptance. When treatment is presented using clinical jargon, fear-based language, or blunt directives — *"you need a crown," "you could lose the tooth," "it's going to get worse"* — patients shut down. Not because they don't care about their health. Because they feel alarmed rather than informed, pressured rather than supported. Case acceptance is not a closing skill. It is a communication skill. And practices that treat it as the former and ignore the latter will always struggle with it.

Patient retention. Patients leave practices for reasons they rarely share out loud. They don't call to complain. They don't write a cancellation letter. They simply don't rebook. And when asked — if they are ever asked — the reason is almost never clinical. It is almost always emotional. They felt dismissed. They felt judged. They felt like a transaction. The words that created that feeling were probably spoken without a second thought by someone who was simply having a busy day.

Reactivation. Calling an overdue patient and leading with *"you're overdue for your cleaning"* is the communication equivalent of opening a conversation with an accusation. It creates shame and defensiveness — the two emotions least likely to result in a scheduled appointment. Yet this is how the majority of reactivation calls in this country are made, every single day.

Referrals. Maya Angelou said it better than anyone ever has:

"People will forget what you said. People will forget what you did. But people will never forget how you made them feel."

Referrals are not generated by clinical excellence alone. They are generated by the feeling a patient carries with them when they leave your practice. That feeling is created — or destroyed — by the language your team uses from the first phone call to the final goodbye at checkout.

It Is Not the Team's Fault

Before we go any further I want to say something clearly — because it matters both for how you read this book and for how you lead your practice through the changes it will ask of you.

Your team is not the problem.

Michelle — the front desk coordinator who told the new patient caller that fees couldn't be given over the phone — is not a bad employee. She is not indifferent. She is not trying to cost the practice patients or revenue. She is a hardworking person who was never given the language to do better. She was hired, shown where the phones were, handed a schedule, and expected to figure out the rest through osmosis and observation.

In most dental practices, communication training begins and ends with "just be friendly."

That is not a strategy. That is a wish.

John Maxwell makes a distinction that I have carried with me throughout my entire career working with dental teams. He says:

"The pessimist complains about the wind. The optimist expects it to change. The leader adjusts the sails."

The wind in your practice is the communication gap. Complaining about it — or hoping it fixes itself — will not fill your schedule or improve your case acceptance. Adjusting the sails means giving your team the specific, intentional, practiced language that transforms every patient interaction from a gamble into a strength.

That is what this book is about.

That is what A.L.I.G.N.™ was built to do.

What Changes When the Words Change

I want to leave you with a picture before we move forward — not of a problem, but of a possibility.

Imagine the same Tuesday morning. The same busy front desk. The same phone ringing on line two. The same woman calling for the first time, a little nervous, asking the same question:

"Hi, I was just wondering — how much is a cleaning and exam?"

This time, the response is different.

"I'd be happy to help you with that. Every patient's needs are a little different, so what I'd love to do is get you scheduled for a visit so we can give you a clear picture of exactly what to expect — and make sure we reserve the right amount of time just for you. How does your schedule look this week?"

Same practice. Same front desk coordinator. Same Tuesday morning.

Different words.

The woman on the phone exhales slightly. She feels heard. She feels like this practice actually wants her there. She schedules the appointment.

She becomes a patient.

She stays for eleven years. She refers her husband, her two children, and her mother. She leaves a five-star review that three other new patients mention when they call.

All of that — from a single sentence spoken differently.

That is not an exaggeration. That is the compounding power of intentional language, played out over the lifetime of a patient relationship. And it is available to every practice, every team member, every phone call — starting right now.

"Small disciplines repeated with consistency every day lead to great achievements gained slowly over time." — John Maxwell

The discipline we are building together — one conversation at a time — is the discipline of intentional, trust-building, connection-first communication.

And it starts with the very next word your team speaks.

Chapter Takeaway

The most expensive problems in most dental practices are not clinical — they are conversational. Poor communication costs practices new patients, case acceptance, retention, reactivation, and referrals — often without anyone realizing it is happening. The solution is not blame. It is awareness, intentional language, and a system that gives every team member the words to build trust at every single touchpoint. That system is A.L.I.G.N.™ — and it starts here.

What This Means for Your Practice

I have walked into a lot of dental practices over 38 years. And the one thing that never changes — regardless of the size of the practice, the market, the demographics, the production goals — is this. The gap between what the team thinks they are communicating and what the patient actually hears is almost always larger than anyone inside the practice realizes.

That gap is not the team's fault. It is nobody's fault. It is the natural result of familiarity — of hearing the same phrases so many times that they stop registering as choices and start feeling like simply how things are done here.

But familiarity does not make a phrase harmless. And the phrases I described in this chapter are costing your practice real patients with real lifetime value every single week.

-Here's What I Want You to Remember-

Here is what I want you to do before you read another page. Think about the last time a new patient called your practice. Think about what the person who answered that phone said in the first thirty seconds. Think about what the patient experienced in those thirty seconds.

If you are not completely certain the answer is warmth, genuine curiosity, and a clear invitation to take the next step — keep reading.

Because the fix is closer than you think.

Chapter 2

The Team Is Not the Problem. The Training Is.

"A leader's job is not to do the work for others, it's to help others figure out how to do it themselves, to get things done, and to succeed beyond what they thought possible." — John Maxwell

There is a conversation that happens in dental practices more often than most practice owners would like to admit. It usually takes place behind closed doors, after a difficult day, in hushed and frustrated tones. It goes something like this:

"I just don't understand why they can't get it right. I've told them a hundred times how I want patients to be greeted. I've explained how the phone should be answered. I've shown them how to handle the insurance questions. And yet every time I turn around it's the same thing. The same mistakes. The same complaints. I'm starting to think I just have the wrong people."

The dentist — or the office manager — saying these words is not wrong to be frustrated. The practice is underperforming. Patients are having inconsistent experiences. The team is not communicating the way leadership imagined they would when they were hired.

But here is where the diagnosis goes wrong.

The assumption underneath that frustration — *I have the wrong people* — is almost never correct. In nearly every case the people are fine. More than fine. They are capable, caring, and genuinely motivated to do good work. What they do not have is a system. What they were never given is training. What nobody ever handed them is the specific, practical, repeatable language that turns good intentions into great patient experiences.

The problem is not the team.

The problem is that the team was handed a headset and a smile and told to figure it out.

"The growth and development of people is the highest calling of leadership." — John Maxwell

Hired for Skill. Left to Wing It.

Think about how most dental team members learn to communicate with patients.

The scheduling coordinator watched the person before her and copied what she saw. The dental assistant learned chairside manner by absorbing whatever the doctor modeled — consciously or not. The hygienist developed her patient communication style through trial and error over years of appointments, keeping what seemed to work and quietly abandoning what didn't. The front desk team member who handles financial conversations learned to talk about money by listening to how the last financial coordinator did it — who learned from the one before her.

This is not training. This is an unbroken chain of inherited habits — some good, many mediocre, some genuinely harmful to the patient relationship — passed down from one generation of dental team members to the next without anyone ever stopping to examine whether any of it actually works.

And layered on top of all of it is the universal instruction given to every dental team member at every practice in every city in this country:

Just be friendly.

Friendly is not nothing. Warmth matters. A genuine smile matters. Making a patient feel welcomed the moment they walk through the door matters enormously. But friendly is not a communication strategy. Friendly does not tell a scheduling coordinator what to say when a patient calls to cancel for the third time this month. Friendly does not tell a hygienist how to respond when a patient pushes back on a periodontal therapy recommendation. Friendly does not tell a front desk coordinator how to present a $4,000 treatment estimate in a way that feels supportive rather than transactional.

Friendly is the starting point. Language is the system that turns that starting point into consistent, trust-building, practice-growing communication.

Without the system, every team member is winging it. And winging it — no matter how warmly — is costing your practice every single day.

The Myth of Natural Talent

Here is something that gets said about communication in dental practices that drives me absolutely crazy:

"Oh, Sarah is just a natural with patients."

Said with admiration. Said as though Sarah's ability to connect with patients, calm their nerves, handle their objections, and send them out the door feeling great about their visit is some kind of gift she was born with — like perfect pitch or the ability to wiggle her ears.

Sarah is not a natural. Sarah has — through years of experience, personal reflection, and probably a fair amount of painful trial and error — developed a set of communication habits that work. She has learned, consciously or unconsciously, how to read a patient's emotional state and respond to it. She has figured out which words open people up and which ones shut them down. She has built a personal language system that serves her patients well.

The problem is that Sarah's system lives entirely inside Sarah's head.

When Sarah goes on vacation the patient experience drops noticeably. When Sarah eventually moves on — and everyone eventually moves on — her replacement starts from scratch, inheriting nothing but the headset and the smile.

John Maxwell addresses this directly when he writes:

"A leader who produces other leaders multiplies their influences."

The goal of A.L.I.G.N.™ is to take what Sarah knows intuitively — what every great dental communicator has figured out through experience — and turn it into a teachable, learnable, repeatable system that any team member can access from day one. Not to replace Sarah's natural warmth. To give everyone on the team the same foundation she built over years — in a fraction of the time.

That is what a real communication training system does. It democratizes excellence.

What Happens When Every Team Member Speaks a Different Language

One of the most damaging and least discussed problems in dental practice communication is inconsistency.

Not the dramatic inconsistency of one team member being rude and another being warm. The subtler, more insidious inconsistency of every team member handling the same situation slightly differently — with no shared language, no agreed-upon approach, and no common understanding of what the practice actually sounds like to a patient moving through it.

A new patient calls and speaks to Jennifer at the front desk. Jennifer is upbeat, solution-oriented, and makes the caller feel genuinely welcome. The patient schedules and arrives for her appointment feeling good about the practice.

At checkout she speaks to Marcus, who is efficient and professional but handles her insurance question with a clipped *"your insurance doesn't cover that"* and moves on to the next patient.

On her way out she passes the hygienist who mentions she should *"really be coming in more often"* without explaining why.

Three interactions. Three completely different emotional experiences. Three different versions of what this practice is.

The patient leaves with a muddled impression. Not bad enough to never return. Not good enough to refer anyone. Somewhere in the foggy middle where most patients who eventually drift away from a practice live for a while before they quietly disappear.

As John Maxwell writes:

"Teamwork makes the dream work, but a vision becomes a nightmare when the leader has a big dream and a bad team."

The team in this scenario is not bad. They are untrained and un A.L.I.G.N.™ ed. There is no shared language. There is no agreed standard for how this practice communicates. And so each team member defaults to their own instincts — which vary as widely as personalities do.

The patient pays the price. So does the practice.

The Real Cost of Winging It

Let's be specific about what communication inconsistency actually costs a practice — because the numbers have a way of making abstract problems feel very concrete very quickly.

New patient conversion. Industry data consistently shows that dental practices convert somewhere between 50 and 70 percent of new patient phone inquiries into scheduled appointments — on a good day. Practices with intentional, trained phone communication convert significantly higher. The difference between a 55 percent conversion rate and a 75 percent conversion rate — on just ten new patient calls per week — is roughly one additional new patient per week. Fifty new patients per year. At a conservative lifetime value of $2,000 per patient that is $100,000 in lifetime production — from phone skills alone.

Case acceptance. The national average for case acceptance in dental practices hovers around 60 percent. Practices where teams are trained in empathetic, education-based treatment communication routinely achieve 75 to 85 percent. The difference is not the quality of the dentistry. It is the quality of the conversation around it.

Staff turnover. This one surprises people. Communication training reduces staff turnover. When team members have clear language systems, consistent expectations, and the tools to handle difficult patient interactions confidently, their job satisfaction improves measurably. They feel capable instead of anxious. They feel supported instead of thrown to the wolves. And team members who feel capable and supported stay longer — saving the practice the $15,000 to $25,000 it costs on average to replace a single dental team member.

All of this from training. All of this from giving your team the words.

"Nobody Ever Taught Me"

I want to share something that I hear with remarkable consistency when I work with dental teams — not from struggling team members but from good ones. From the Sarahs of the world. From the coordinators and hygienists and assistants who are doing their jobs well and genuinely care about the patients they serve.

When I ask them — in training sessions, in one-on-one conversations, in group workshops — what they wish someone had taught them earlier in their career, the answer is almost always a version of the same thing.

"Nobody ever taught me what to say when a patient tells me they're terrified. I just said 'don't worry, you'll be fine' and hoped for the best."

"Nobody ever taught me how to talk about money without feeling like I was asking for something I shouldn't be asking for."

"Nobody ever taught me how to handle the patient who pushes back on treatment. I would just kind of agree with them and then feel terrible about it afterward."

"Nobody ever taught me how to call a patient who hasn't been in for two years without making them feel guilty."

Nobody ever taught them.

Not because the practices they worked for didn't care. Because nobody in the dental industry had ever built a system specifically designed to teach these things — clearly, practically, and in the language of the dental practice itself.

That gap is what A.L.I.G.N.™ was built to fill.

Brené Brown writes:

"Connection is why we're here. It is what gives purpose and meaning to our lives."

Every one of those team members who said *"nobody ever taught me"* was describing a missed connection. A moment where a patient needed to feel heard and supported, and the team member wanted desperately to provide that — but didn't have the words. The desire was there. The training was not.

When you give people the words, the connections happen. And when the connections happen consistently, across every team member, at every touchpoint, the practice transforms.

Training Is Not a One-Time Event

Before we close this chapter I want to address something that comes up in almost every practice I work with — the idea that communication training is something you do once and check off the list.

A staff meeting. A workshop. A guest speaker at the annual team retreat. These are valuable starting points — and for most practices they are exactly that. A starting point. The energy is real. The content is good. The intention is genuine. What is missing is not the event itself but the system that sustains what the event ignites.

This is not a failure of the team. This is a failure of the training model.

John Maxwell is unambiguous on this point:

"You cannot push anyone up the ladder unless they are willing to climb themselves."

And I would add — you cannot expect anyone to climb a ladder they can only see once. Real communication training is ongoing. It is woven into the daily rhythm of the practice. It is revisited in morning huddles. It is reinforced in team meetings. It is modeled by leadership in every interaction. It is built into onboarding so that every new team member starts with the same foundation rather than inheriting the habits of whoever sat in that chair before them.

That is the difference between training and culture.

Training is an event. Culture is a system.

A.L.I.G.N.™ is built to be a system — one that begins with the kind of genuine inspiration a great seminar or workshop produces and then gives that inspiration somewhere to go. A place to land. A daily structure that keeps it alive long after the energy of any single event would naturally fade. It is a living, breathing communication framework that grows with your practice, adapts to your challenges, and gets stronger the more consistently it is used.

The team is not the problem. They never were.

Give them the system. Give them the language. Give them the training they deserve from day one and watch what they do with it.

You will not be disappointed.

Chapter Takeaway

Most dental teams are not failing at communication — they are simply winging it, having inherited a chain of habits nobody ever stopped to examine. The solution is not better people. It is better training — specific, practical, repeatable language systems that turn good intentions into consistent, trust-building patient experiences. Communication excellence is not a natural talent reserved for a gifted few. It is a teachable skill that every team member deserves to be given. A.L.I.G.N.™ exists to give it to them.

What This Means for Your Practice

This chapter exists because of something I have watched happen too many times. A dentist sits across from me — genuinely, understandably frustrated — and says some version of the same thing. I just do not think I have the right people.

And I have to tell them the truth.

You probably have exactly the right people. What you do not have yet is the right system.

I have never walked into a dental practice and found a team full of people who did not care. What I have found — consistently, in practice after practice across 38 years — is capable, caring people who were handed a desk and a smile and told to figure out the communication part on their own.

That is not a people problem. That is a training problem. And training problems are completely solvable.

-Here's What I Want You to Remember-

Your team is not failing you. They are waiting for someone to give them what they deserve — specific, practical, immediately applicable language tools that match the genuine care they already bring to this work every single day.

That is what this book is giving them. Trust them with it.

Chapter 3

Why Great Training Deserves a Great System

"People buy into the leader before they buy into the vision." — John Maxwell

There is a particular kind of hope that lives in the heart of a dentist who has decided to invest in practice management coaching.

It usually arrives after a long stretch of frustration. The schedule is unpredictable. Case acceptance feels like a coin flip. The team is doing their best but something is consistently off and nobody can quite put their finger on what it is. The dentist has tried the usual fixes — a new software system, a different insurance mix, a staff meeting that everyone left feeling vaguely motivated for approximately forty-eight hours.

And then someone — a colleague at a study club, a vendor at a dental conference, an ad in a trade publication — mentions a coaching program. A consultant. A practice management system that promises to change everything.

The dentist signs up. The investment is significant — sometimes tens of thousands of dollars. The commitment is real. The hope is genuine.

And sometimes it works. Partially. For a while.

But often — more often than the coaching industry would like to acknowledge — something feels off about the process. The metrics improve on paper. The production numbers tick upward. But the culture feels strained. The team feels pressured. And the dentist, who got into dentistry because they wanted to help people, finds themselves wondering when exactly their practice started feeling less like a place of care and more like a sales floor.

That feeling is not a coincidence.

It is the natural result of a coaching model built on the wrong foundation.

"Leadership is not about the next election, it's about the next generation." — John Maxwell

The Production-First Model

The dominant model in dental practice coaching for the past several decades has been built around a single organizing principle:

Increase production per hour.

Everything flows from that number. See fewer patients. Charge more per visit. Focus on high-fee elective cases. Reduce dependence on insurance. Work less. Earn more.

There is nothing inherently wrong with any of those goals in isolation. Profitability matters. Sustainable scheduling matters. Reducing burnout matters enormously in a profession with one of the highest rates of occupational stress of any healthcare field.

The problem is not the destination. The problem is the road the production-first model takes to get there — and what it asks of the team along the way.

When production per hour becomes the organizing principle of a practice, everything else — including the patient relationship — gets evaluated through that lens. Patient interactions become conversion opportunities. Treatment presentations become closing exercises. The front desk coordinator stops being a patient advocate and starts being a gatekeeper for high-value appointments. The hygienist stops being a health educator and starts being a case generator.

And patients feel it.

They may not be able to name it. They may not walk out of the practice and say *"that felt like a sales pitch."* But something registers. A slight pressure behind the treatment presentation. A subtle urgency in the financial conversation. A feeling that the practice is more interested in what they can produce than what they need.

Seth Godin captures it perfectly:

"Marketing is no longer about the stuff that you make, but about the stories you tell."

The story a production-first practice tells — whether it intends to or not — is that the patient is a means to an end. And that story, told consistently through language, tone, and behavior, erodes the very trust that a thriving practice depends on.

When Scripts Replace Connection

One of the most common tools in the production-first coaching toolkit is the script.

Not guidance. Not principles. Not a framework for thinking about patient communication. An actual word-for-word script — memorized, rehearsed, and deployed on patients with the precision of a sales funnel.

Scripts have a seductive appeal. They feel like a solution. They take the anxiety out of difficult conversations by replacing the need to think with the comfort of a pre-written response. Team members feel more confident. Leadership feels more in control. And in the short term, the numbers often do improve.

But here is what scripts cannot do:

They cannot replace genuine empathy. They cannot adapt to the individual human being sitting in the chair. They cannot survive the moment when a patient says something unexpected and the team member's eyes go slightly blank while they search their mental script library for the appropriate response.

And patients notice.

Brené Brown writes:

"Authenticity is the daily practice of letting go of who we think we're supposed to be and embracing who we are."

A team member reciting a memorized script is the opposite of authentic. They are performing a version of connection rather than experiencing it. And the patient — who came to the practice hoping to feel cared for — receives a performance instead of a relationship.

The irony is profound. The script was designed to improve the patient experience. Instead it hollows it out.

This is not to say that language guidance has no value — this entire book is built on the premise that the words matter enormously. But there is a fundamental difference between giving a team member a script to recite and giving them a principle to understand. One replaces thinking. The other deepens it. One fades the moment the situation deviates from what the script anticipated. The other grows stronger with every conversation.

The Hidden Cost of Turning Caregivers into Salespeople

There is a human cost to the production-first model that rarely appears in the practice management conversation — and it sits squarely with the team.

Dental team members, by and large, chose their careers because they wanted to help people. The front desk coordinator who lights up when a nervous patient leaves the office smiling chose that job because human connection matters to her. The hygienist who spends 45 to 60 minutes not just cleaning teeth but genuinely listening to a patient's concerns about their health chose that career because caring for people is who she is.

When a coaching program reframes her role — explicitly or implicitly — as a case generator, something breaks a little.

She starts to feel like she is being asked to be someone she is not. The conversations that used to feel natural start to feel scripted and pressured. She begins to dread the patients who push back on treatment because she knows she is expected to overcome their objections rather than genuinely address their concerns. She starts counting down to the end of her shift in a way she never used to.

And then one day she updates her resume.

John Maxwell speaks directly to this when he writes:

"A great leader's courage to fulfill his vision comes from passion, not position."

When you strip the passion out of a team member's role by turning it into a sales function, you do not just lose their enthusiasm. You eventually lose them entirely. And the cost of replacing a single dental team member — in recruiting time, training investment, and the inevitable dip in patient experience during the transition — is significant by any measure.

The production-first model often improves short-term revenue while quietly degrading the team culture that makes long-term growth possible. It is a trade that looks good on a quarterly report and feels hollow in the hallway.

What Patients Are Really Looking For

Here is something the production-first model consistently underestimates:

Patients are not primarily looking for a great deal. They are not primarily looking for the most advanced technology or the longest list of services. They are not even primarily looking for the most technically skilled dentist in town — though skill obviously matters.

What patients are primarily looking for is someone they trust.

Trust that the practice sees them as a person, not a production unit. Trust that the treatment being recommended is genuinely in their best interest. Trust that when they share their fear, their financial concern, or their hesitation, they will be met with understanding rather than a rebuttal.

Dale Carnegie identified this truth nearly a century ago and it has not changed:

"You can make more friends in two months by becoming interested in other people than you can in two years by trying to get other people interested in you."

The dental practices that grow sustainably — that build waitlists of new patients, that have hygiene schedules booked three months out, that generate referrals without ever asking for them — are not the practices with the most aggressive case presentation systems. They are the practices where patients feel genuinely seen, heard, and cared for.

That feeling is not manufactured by a script. It is not produced by a closing technique. It is created — consistently, reliably, and scalably — by a team that has been trained to communicate from a foundation of authentic connection.

That is a fundamentally different starting point than production per hour.

And it produces fundamentally different results.

The Weekend Retreat Problem

There is one more aspect of the traditional coaching model worth examining before we move forward — not because it is dishonest, but because it is structurally incapable of producing the kind of lasting change it promises.

The weekend retreat.

Or the two-day intensive. Or the quarterly consultant visit. Or the annual conference where everyone gets fired up, fills a notebook with ideas, comes home exhausted and inspired, and returns to exactly the same practice doing exactly the same things within two weeks.

This is not a failure of motivation. It is a failure of implementation architecture.

Real change — the kind that sticks, the kind that becomes culture, the kind that a new hire absorbs on their first day because it is simply how things are done here — does not happen in a weekend. It happens in the daily repetition of small, intentional habits reinforced over time.

John Maxwell has written extensively about this principle:

"You'll never change your life until you change something you do daily. The secret of your success is found in your daily routine."

A coaching model built around periodic intensive events is asking a practice to change its life without changing its daily routine. It is the organizational equivalent of crash dieting — dramatic results in the short term, slow regression to baseline as soon as the external pressure is removed.

A.L.I.G.N.™ was designed with this reality in mind. It is not a retreat. It is not an intensive. It is a system that lives in the daily rhythm of the practice — in the morning huddle, in the way new team members are onboarded, in the language that leadership models every single day. It grows stronger with use rather than fading between visits.

A Different Foundation

So what does a coaching model built on the right foundation look like?

It starts with the patient relationship rather than the production number. It measures success not just by revenue per hour but by trust, retention, case acceptance born of genuine understanding, and a team culture where people want to come to work.

It trains for principles rather than scripts — giving team members the understanding to navigate any patient interaction rather than the memorized response to navigate a predictable one.

It builds systems that outlast any individual — so that when Sarah goes on vacation or eventually moves on, the practice communicates just as consistently and just as warmly as it did when she was there.

It treats the team as the most valuable asset in the practice — not because that is a nice thing to say, but because it is demonstrably true. No technology, no marketing budget, no office renovation produces results that a well-trained, genuinely connected team produces every single day.

And it understands that the goal is not a better-producing practice. The goal is a better practice — one that produces more because it serves better, connects deeper, and communicates with the kind of authenticity that patients recognize, respond to, and remember.

Simon Sinek puts it this way:

"People don't buy what you do; they buy why you do it."

The why of A.L.I.G.N.™ is not production. It is not revenue per hour. It is not case acceptance percentages — though all of those improve when the system is working.

The why is this: every patient who walks into a dental practice deserves to be met by a team that communicates with genuine care, clear confidence, and the kind of language that builds trust rather than transactions.

When that happens consistently — across every team member, every touchpoint, every conversation — the practice does not just improve.

It transforms.

Chapter Takeaway

The dominant dental coaching model is built around production metrics and uses scripted persuasion techniques that can pressure patients and demoralize teams. Real, lasting practice transformation requires a different foundation — one that starts with the patient relationship, trains for principles rather than scripts, builds culture rather than compliance, and treats consistent daily language habits as the highest-leverage tool in the practice. That is the foundation A.L.I.G.N.™ is built on — and it is why it produces results that outlast any weekend retreat or quarterly consultant visit.

What This Means for Your Practice

I want to be honest with you about something.

Every workshop I have ever facilitated. Every team training day. Every coaching session that left the room energized and committed and genuinely ready to do things differently — I have watched the energy of every single one of them meet the reality of Monday morning.

Not because the training was bad. Because training without a system is inspiration without a home.

The inspiration is real. The intention is genuine. And without the daily huddle, the monthly review, the onboarding system, and the specific language practice that keeps new habits alive — the inspiration finds nowhere to land and the old habits quietly reclaim the space it briefly occupied.

"Here's What I Want You to Remember"

I am not asking you to abandon the training investments you have already made. I am asking you to protect them — with the systems that keep them working long after the day they were delivered.

A.L.I.G.N.™ is that protection. It is what makes every communication investment your practice has ever made finally produce the lasting results it always deserved to produce.

The Foundation Behind A.L.I.G.N.™

How Three Decades Inside Dental Practices Built a Framework

Before we go any further I want you to understand something important about what you are about to learn.

A.L.I.G.N.™ was not created in a boardroom. It was not developed from theory, trends, or the latest business book. It was not built by someone who studied dental practices from the outside.

It was born from decades of real experience inside them.

Since 1988 dentistry has been my classroom. Every success, every challenge, every mistake, every breakthrough, every leadership lesson, and every patient interaction contributed to what you are holding in your hands right now. I began as a dental assistant — chairside, in the operatory, learning the clinical rhythm of a practice from the ground up. I moved into office management. I trained dental teams on software across the country. And for the past twenty years I have been coaching practices — sitting with dentists, office managers, and their teams — trying to understand why some practices thrive and others struggle despite having every resource they need to succeed.

What I discovered changed everything I thought I knew about dental practice growth.

Understanding Misalignment

For years the dental consulting world focused on the same familiar list.

Production. Collections. New patient numbers. Case acceptance rates. Schedule density. Marketing spend. Software upgrades. Equipment investments.

When results declined the response was predictable — more marketing, better software, a new consultant, another seminar, or the quiet conclusion that the problem was simply the wrong people on the team.

I watched this pattern repeat itself in practice after practice. And I kept asking the same question.

If the systems are right and the metrics are being tracked and the team has been trained — why is nothing permanently changing?

The answer was always the same. And it was never the answer anyone expected.

The practices that were struggling were not underperforming because of their systems. They were underperforming because of misalignment. They were:

Disconnected — from each other and from the patients they served.

Reactive — responding to problems rather than preventing them.

Inconsistent — delivering different experiences depending on who answered the phone or who handled the checkout.

Unclear — about who they were as a practice and what they stood for.

Fragmented — with leadership, team, and systems all pulling in different directions.

Many practices operate in this state without realizing it. Because when you are inside it the misalignment feels like simply how things are. It does not feel like a problem that has a name. It feels like Tuesday.

Discovering Alignment

Alignment is different.

Not different in theory — different in practice. Different in the daily experience of the team, the patient, and the leader who is responsible for sustaining the culture that produces genuine long-term growth.

Aligned practices are:

Connected — to each other, to their patients, and to a shared understanding of who they are.

Intentional — about how they communicate, how they lead, and how they develop the people in their care.

Consistent — delivering the same excellent experience whether Tammy is in the building or not.

Clear — about their identity, their values, and the standard they hold themselves to.

Integrated — with leadership, language, and systems working together rather than independently.

Over time I came to understand something that changed the way I coach, the way I train, and the way I think about dental practice growth entirely.

The difference between a thriving practice and a struggling one was almost never the scheduling system. It was almost never the software or the marketing campaign or the equipment investment.

The difference was leadership.

The difference was communication.

The difference was accountability.

The difference was ownership.

The difference was creating an environment where people understood their purpose, their impact, and their responsibility to one another — and were given the specific language and the daily systems to express all three in every patient interaction.

A.L.I.G.N.™ reorganizes everything through that lens.

Not results first. Not numbers first. Not systems first.

People first. Leadership first. Communication first.

The goal is not to find the right team. The goal is to develop stronger leaders who build stronger teams — teams that communicate effectively, take ownership, hold themselves accountable, and work together toward a shared vision.

My Journey to A.L.I.G.N.™

This book is deeply personal. Because it was created through my own journey of growth and awareness.

I know what it feels like to not know what you do not know.

I know what it feels like to work hard, chase results, solve problems, and still feel like something is missing — like the improvement is real but somehow fragile, dependent on the right conditions and the right people and the right week rather than on something genuinely sustainable.

A.L.I.G.N.™ is the result of 38 years of observation, implementation, coaching, leadership, and personal transformation. It represents a shift from managing outcomes to leading people. From fixing problems to creating awareness. From reacting to responding with intention. From misalignment to alignment.

Without those years of experience — without the practices that trusted me enough to let me sit with their teams and their challenges and their genuine desire to build something better — I would not be able to share what I know today.

My hope is that this framework gives you new lenses through which to see your practice, your team, your leadership, and ultimately yourself.

Because when people become aligned — truly aligned, in the way this book describes — everything else begins to align as well.

The language gets better. The culture gets stronger. The metrics move. The patients feel the difference. And the team that was always capable of excellence finally has the system that makes excellence sustainable.

That is what A.L.I.G.N.™ was built to do.

Now let us talk about how it works.

What This Means for Your Practice

I want to be honest about something that took me years to fully articulate.

The practices I have watched struggle most consistently were not struggling because they lacked talent, commitment, or resources. They were struggling because the talent, the commitment, and the resources were all pulling in slightly different directions — and nobody had ever named that as the problem.

Misalignment is quiet. It does not announce itself. It shows up as a cancellation rate that will not move, a team that trains well and reverts immediately, a dentist who cannot understand why the culture feels off when everything on paper looks right.

Naming it changes everything. Because you cannot fix what you cannot see.

Here's What I Want You to Remember

Before you read another chapter I want you to sit with one question.

Is your practice operating from alignment or misalignment right now?

Not as a judgment. As an honest assessment. Because the answer to that question — held honestly, without defensiveness — is the foundation on which everything in this book builds.

A.L.I.G.N.™ begins with seeing clearly. And seeing clearly begins right here.

Chapter 4

What Is A.L.I.G.N.™?

"A dream is just a dream. A goal is a dream with a plan and a deadline."
— John Maxwell

Every great solution has an origin story.

This one starts with a question.

Not a dramatic question. Not a question asked in a boardroom or a conference hall or a moment of sudden revelation. A quiet question — the kind that grows slowly in the back of your mind over months and years of watching the same problem play out in practice after practice, city after city, team after team.

The question was this:

Why does the same conversation produce such different results in different practices?

Two practices. Same city. Similar demographics. Comparable clinical quality. One has a waitlist for new patients, a hygiene schedule booked three months out, and a team that has worked together for an average of seven years. The other struggles to fill the schedule, loses new patients before they ever become patients, and has turned over half its team in the last two years.

The difference is not the dentistry. The difference is not the technology or the location or the marketing budget.

The difference — almost without exception — is the communication.

Not just the words. The thinking behind the words. The culture that shapes the words. The systems that make the words consistent. The leadership that models the words every single day.

That is where A.L.I.G.N.™ was born. Not from a theory. From a pattern observed so consistently, in so many practices, over so many years, that it became impossible to ignore — and irresponsible not to address.

"The whole is greater than the sum of its parts." — Aristotle, cited frequently by John Maxwell

More Than a Communication Tool

The first thing most people assume when they encounter A.L.I.G.N.™ is that it is a communication training program.

That assumption is understandable. Communication is where A.L.I.G.N.™ is most visible. It is where the changes are most immediately felt — by patients, by team members, and by practice owners watching their schedule fill and their case acceptance climb.

But A.L.I.G.N.™ is not just a communication tool. It is a complete practice transformation system that uses communication as its entry point — because communication is the most visible, most measurable, and most immediately changeable aspect of how a practice operates.

Think of it this way.

A dental practice is an ecosystem. Every part of it affects every other part. The way the phone is answered affects whether new patients schedule. Whether new patients schedule affects the hygiene recare system. The hygiene recare system affects treatment diagnosis and presentation. Treatment presentation affects case acceptance. Case acceptance affects production. Production affects team compensation and morale. Team morale affects how the phone is answered.

It is a circle. And the fastest, most leverage-rich place to enter that circle — the place where a change produces the most downstream impact most quickly — is communication.

Change the words and you begin to change the culture. Change the culture and you begin to change the systems. Change the systems and you begin to change the outcomes. Change the outcomes and you change the practice.

That is the A.L.I.G.N.™ logic. And it works because it is not imposed from the outside — it grows from the inside out, from the daily language habits of every single person on the team.

The "Instead Of" Philosophy

Before we walk through the five pillars of A.L.I.G.N.™ I want to spend a moment on the philosophy at the heart of the system — because understanding it changes how you read everything that follows.

The "Instead Of" principle is built on a simple but powerful insight about human behavior:

Contrast is the fastest path to awareness.

You can tell someone that their communication needs to improve. You can explain the principles of empathetic language. You can lecture on the neuroscience of trust and the psychology of patient behavior. All of that is valuable. None of it produces change as quickly or as viscerally as showing someone the exact phrase they are currently using — and placing directly next to it the phrase they should be using instead.

Instead of "We can't give fees over the phone" — say "I'd be happy to help you understand what to expect and reserve time for your visit."

In that moment of contrast something clicks. The team member does not just understand the principle intellectually. They feel the difference. They hear the wall go up in one phrase and the door open in the other. They recognize — often with a wince of uncomfortable familiarity — that they have been saying the wall phrase for years without realizing what it was doing.

That recognition is the beginning of real change.

John Maxwell writes:

"Awareness is the first step toward change. You cannot fix what you cannot see."

The "Instead Of" framework makes the invisible visible. It shows people exactly where the communication is breaking down and gives them the replacement language immediately — so there is no gap between awareness and action. They do not leave the training thinking *"I need to communicate better."* They leave knowing precisely what to say differently and why it matters.

That immediacy is what makes the system work in the real world of a busy dental practice — where there is no time for lengthy philosophical reflection between phone calls.

The Five Pillars of A.L.I.G.N.™

Now let us walk through the system itself.

A.L.I.G.N.™ stands for five things. Five pillars that each address a distinct dimension of practice performance — and that together form a complete framework for sustainable growth.

They are not sequential steps. They are simultaneous forces. A practice that works on Language without Awareness is improving words without understanding why they need to change. A practice that sets Goals without Identity has numbers without culture. A practice that builds Navigation systems without Language has infrastructure without the human connection that fills it.

All five work together. All five reinforce each other. And all five are accessible to every practice — regardless of size, market, or current performance level.

A — Awareness *You cannot fix what you cannot see*

Awareness is the foundation of everything that follows in the A.L.I.G.N.™ system — because without it, all the language training and goal-setting in the world is aimed in the wrong direction.

Awareness in the context of A.L.I.G.N.™ means developing a clear, honest, unsentimental picture of where the practice currently stands — not just financially, but communicatively. It means identifying the revenue gaps and blind spots that are hiding in plain sight. The phone calls that are not converting. The treatment plans that are not being accepted. The patients who are not returning. The team interactions that are subtly undermining the patient relationship without anyone realizing it.

Most practices have a general sense that something is off. Awareness turns that general sense into specific knowledge — and specific knowledge is the only kind you can actually act on.

As John Maxwell writes:

"The first step to achieving your goal is to take a moment to respect your goal. Know what it means to you to achieve it."

You cannot respect a goal you cannot clearly see. Awareness gives you the clear sight.

L — Language *The right words at the right moment change everything*

Language is the most visible pillar of A.L.I.G.N.™ and the one that produces the most immediate results — which is why it tends to be where most practices want to start.

Language in the A.L.I.G.N.™ framework is not about scripts or sales techniques. It is about developing a shared communication vocabulary across the entire team — a common language of care, confidence, and connection that every team member speaks regardless of their role, their personality, or their experience level.

It covers every touchpoint. The first phone call. The new patient greeting. The treatment presentation. The financial conversation. The confirmation call. The reactivation outreach. The checkout experience. Every moment where a word is spoken is a moment where trust is either built or eroded — and Language training ensures that every one of those moments is working for the practice rather than against it.

John Maxwell is direct about the power of words in leadership:

"The most important words you will ever speak are the ones you say to yourself and others every day."

In a dental practice those words are spoken hundreds of times a day. A.L.I.G.N.™ ensures they are the right ones.

I — Identity *Who your practice IS determines how your practice SPEAKS*

Identity is the pillar that most practice management programs skip entirely — and it is the one that determines whether any of the other changes last.

Identity in the A.L.I.G.N.™ framework operates on two levels.

The first is leadership identity. How the dentist and practice owner sees themselves — not just as a clinician, but as a leader, a culture-setter, a communicator — determines everything that flows from them. Teams mirror their leaders. The language a dentist uses in the hallway becomes the language the team uses at the front desk. The tone a leader sets in the Daily A.L.I.G.N.™ Meeting becomes the emotional temperature of the entire day.

The second is practice identity. Who the practice is — what it stands for, how it treats people, what patients feel when they walk through the door — is not a marketing statement. It is a lived reality created by every interaction, every word, every moment of connection or disconnection between the team and the people they serve.

When leadership identity and practice identity are strong and A.L.I.G.N.™ ed, communication does not feel like training. It feels like expression. Team members are not performing a script. They are being themselves — their best, most intentional selves — in service of something they genuinely believe in.

John Maxwell could not be clearer on this point:

"Everything rises and falls on leadership."

Identity is where leadership lives. And leadership is where everything begins.

G — Goals *Vague goals produce vague results*

Goals in the A.L.I.G.N.™ framework are not just financial targets. They are communication targets — specific, measurable, and directly connected to the language and culture work the practice is doing.

What percentage of new patient calls are converting to scheduled appointments? What is the current case acceptance rate — and what would a ten percent improvement mean in annual production? How many overdue patients are being successfully reactivated each month? How long has the average team member been with the practice?

These numbers tell a story. And when they are tracked alongside the language work — when a practice can see the direct correlation between more intentional communication and better measurable outcomes — the entire team develops a shared investment in the process.

Goals also create accountability. Not the punitive, fear-based accountability of performance improvement plans and quarterly reviews. The positive, growth-oriented accountability of a team that knows where it is going, can see how far it has come, and is genuinely motivated to keep improving.

As John Maxwell writes:

"A goal properly set is halfway reached."

A.L.I.G.N.™ helps practices set the right goals — and gives them the communication tools to reach them.

N — Navigation *Building systems that outlast any one person*

Navigation is the pillar that turns everything the practice has learned and built into something permanent.

It is the answer to the question every practice owner eventually asks: *"How do I make sure this sticks?"*

Navigation means building the systems, structures, and processes that embed A.L.I.G.N.™ language and culture into the DNA of the practice — so that it does not depend on any one person being in the right place on the right day. New team members are onboarded into it. Morning huddles reinforce it. Performance conversations reference it. The practice grows and evolves with it rather than outgrowing it.

Navigation is what separates a trained team from a system-dependent practice. And a system-dependent practice is the only kind that produces long-term, predictable growth regardless of who is on the team or what the market is doing.

John Maxwell writes:

"A leader is one who knows the way, goes the way, and shows the way."

Navigation is the map. And with the right map even a practice that has been wandering for years can find its way to where it has always been capable of going.

How the System Works Together

Here is the beautiful thing about A.L.I.G.N.™ as a complete system:

Each pillar makes the others more powerful.

Awareness without Language gives you knowledge without the tools to act on it. Language without Identity gives you better words spoken by people who do not fully believe them. Identity without Goals gives you a great culture with no clear direction. Goals without Navigation gives you targets with no system to hit them consistently.

But when all five are working together — when a practice has the awareness to see clearly, the language to communicate powerfully, the identity to lead authentically, the goals to measure progress honestly, and the navigation to sustain growth systemically — something remarkable happens.

The practice stops feeling like a series of problems to manage and starts feeling like a living, growing, self-reinforcing system of excellence.

Patients feel it the moment they call. They feel it when they walk in the door. They feel it in the operatory, at checkout, and in the follow-up call three days after their procedure. And that feeling — that consistent, authentic, trust-building feeling — is what turns a dental practice from a place people visit into a place people belong.

This Is Not Theory

I want to be clear about something before we move into the chapters that explore each pillar in depth.

A.L.I.G.N.™ was not developed in a classroom or designed from research papers. It was built in the field — in real practices, with real teams, through real conversations with real patients. Every principle in this system has been tested against the unforgiving reality of a busy dental practice where the phone is ringing, the schedule is full, and nobody has time for anything that does not work immediately and consistently.

The language examples throughout this book are not hypothetical. They are drawn from actual patient interactions — the phrases that hurt and the phrases that heal, observed over years of practice coaching across dozens of practices.

The framework is not abstract. It is practical, specific, and immediately applicable — because a communication system that cannot be used on Monday morning is not a communication system. It is a philosophy. And philosophies alone do not fill schedules.

As John Maxwell reminds us:

"Dreams don't work unless you do."

A.L.I.G.N.™ works because it was built for people who work — for the front desk coordinator juggling three things at once, for the hygienist with fifteen minutes between patients, for the dentist who wants a thriving practice without sacrificing the quality of care or the culture of the team.

It works because it meets people where they are and gives them something they can use right now.

And in the chapters that follow we are going to go deep into each pillar — not just what it means, but how it works, why it matters, and exactly what it looks like when it is alive and functioning inside a real dental practice.

The transformation starts here.

Chapter Takeaway

A.L.I.G.N.™ is not just a communication training program — it is a complete practice transformation system that uses communication as its entry point because communication is the highest-leverage point of change in any dental practice. Built on the "Instead Of" philosophy of contrast-based awareness, it operates across five simultaneous pillars — Awareness, Language, Identity, Goals, and Navigation — each one reinforcing the others to produce lasting cultural change, sustainable growth, and a patient experience that patients feel, remember, and tell others about. It was not built in a classroom. It was built in the field. And it works.

What This Means for Your Practice

I built A.L.I.G.N.™ because I kept seeing the same thing.

Practices that had tried everything. Scripts. Training days. New hire orientation checklists. Communication workshops. All of it producing some improvement and none of it producing the kind of deep, permanent, self-sustaining communication culture that the practice — and the team, and the patients — genuinely deserved.

And every time I sat with a practice owner who was frustrated by that pattern I found myself saying the same thing.

You are not missing better training. You are missing a framework. Something that addresses not just what your team says but who they understand themselves to be when they say it. Not just the language but the identity behind the language. Not just the improvement but the systems that make the improvement permanent.

-Here's What I Want You to Remember-

Five pillars. Each one essential. Each one making the others stronger. Together producing something that no single pillar could produce alone — a communication culture that sustains itself because it is built into the daily DNA of how your practice operates.

When you understand why all five pillars are necessary you stop looking for the shortcut. Because you realize the framework is the shortcut.

Chapter 5

A is for Awareness

You Can't Fix What You Can't See

"The greatest mistake we make is living in constant fear that we will make one." — John Maxwell

There is a moment that happens in almost every practice coaching engagement that I have come to think of as the Awareness Moment.

It is not a dramatic moment. There is no thunderclap. No sudden revelation accompanied by soaring music. It is quieter than that — and in many ways more powerful because of its quiet.

It usually happens during a simple exercise. I ask the practice owner or office manager to listen — really listen — to how the phones are being answered. Not to evaluate. Not to critique. Just to listen as if they were a patient calling for the first time.

And somewhere in that listening — usually within the first two or three calls — something shifts behind their eyes.

They hear it.

The slight edge in the voice when an insurance question comes up. The clipped response when a caller asks about pricing. The confirmation call that opens with *"are you still coming tomorrow?"* The front desk coordinator who handles twenty calls a day with genuine warmth and one specific phrase — used reflexively, without thinking — that quietly closes a door every single time.

The practice owner did not know. The office manager did not know. The team member certainly did not know. Nobody was hiding anything. Nobody was being careless on purpose.

They simply could not see what they could not see.

That is where every transformation begins. Not with solutions — with sight.

"We cannot become what we need to be by remaining what we are." — John Maxwell

The Blind Spot Problem

Every dental practice has blind spots.

Not because the people running them are inattentive or incompetent. Because blind spots are, by definition, invisible to the person who has them. They exist precisely in the places where familiarity has replaced objectivity — where something has been done the same way for so long that it no longer registers as a choice. It simply is the way things are done here.

Blind spots in dental practice communication are particularly costly because they live in the highest-traffic moments of the patient experience. They are not hiding in obscure corners of the practice. They are sitting right at the front desk, on the phone lines, in the hygiene room, and at the checkout counter — in the interactions that happen dozens of times every single day.

And because they are invisible to the people experiencing them from the inside, they can persist for years — quietly costing the practice new patients, case acceptance, retention, and referrals — while everyone inside the practice genuinely believes things are going reasonably well.

This is the blind spot problem. And it is more common than anyone in dentistry likes to admit.

Consider these scenarios — each one drawn from real practices, each one representing a blind spot that the team had no idea existed until someone helped them see it:

A scheduling coordinator who genuinely loves her job and her patients ends every confirmation call with *"okay, so we'll see you tomorrow — and if anything comes up just give us a call."* She means it as an accommodation. She is being flexible and understanding. What she does not realize is that she is scripting an exit every single time — planting the suggestion of cancellation in the patient's mind with the phrase *"if anything comes up."* Her cancellation rate is fifteen percent higher than the national average. She has no idea why.

A hygienist who is clinically exceptional and deeply committed to her patients' health delivers her home care recommendations at the end of every appointment with a slight but consistent edge of frustration when patients have not improved since their last visit. She does not think of herself as judgmental. She is not trying to shame anyone. But the patients in her chair feel assessed rather than supported — and her recare retention rate tells the story her intentions cannot see.

A dentist who presents treatment with complete clinical accuracy and genuine concern for his patients consistently uses language that, while technically correct, frames every recommendation in terms of what will happen if the patient does not act. *"If we don't address this it could get significantly worse." "You really don't want to let this go."* He is not wrong. But his patients leave feeling alarmed rather than empowered — and his case acceptance rate sits ten points below where it should be for his skill level and his genuine quality of care.

None of these people are doing anything wrong in the conventional sense. All of them are working hard, caring genuinely, and showing up every day with the best of intentions.

They simply cannot see what their words are doing.

Awareness changes that.

What Awareness Actually Looks Like

In the A.L.I.G.N.™ framework Awareness is not a feeling. It is not a general sense of wanting to do better or a vague acknowledgment that there is room for improvement.

Awareness is specific. It is earned through deliberate observation, honest assessment, and the willingness to look at the practice not through the eyes of someone who works there every day — but through the eyes of a patient experiencing it for the first time.

There are three areas where Awareness work consistently reveals the most significant opportunities in dental practices:

The phone experience. The telephone is the first impression for every new patient — and for many returning patients it is the most frequent touchpoint they have with the practice outside of their actual appointments. Yet it is almost universally the least examined, least trained, and least consistent communication channel in the practice.

When was the last time you listened to how your phones are being answered — not to monitor compliance, but to genuinely evaluate the patient experience from the first hello to the goodbye? When was the last time you called your own practice as a new patient would call and paid attention to how it felt?

Most practice owners have not done this in years. Some have never done it at all.

The phone experience audit is one of the fastest and most revealing awareness exercises available to any practice. It costs nothing. It requires no consultant and no software. It requires only the willingness to listen honestly — and to write down what you hear without defending it.

John Maxwell writes:

"One of the greatest gifts you can give people is the gift of your attention."

The awareness audit is, at its core, an act of attention. You are paying attention to your practice the way your patients experience it — and that attention, honestly applied, reveals more about what needs to change than any amount of data analysis.

The treatment presentation experience. How does your practice present treatment recommendations? Not the clinical content — the communication experience.

Does the patient leave a treatment conversation feeling informed and supported — or alarmed and pressured? Do they understand not just what is recommended but why it matters for their specific health and their specific life? Do they feel that the recommendation is genuinely in their best interest — or do they carry a subtle suspicion that the practice benefits from their saying yes?

These questions cannot be answered by looking at case acceptance numbers alone. A sixty percent case acceptance rate tells you that four out of ten recommended treatment plans are not being accepted. It does not tell you why. Awareness work digs into the why — and almost always finds a communication pattern at the root of it.

The team communication experience. How does your team communicate with each other — and how does that internal communication affect the patient experience?

Teams that communicate poorly internally almost always communicate inconsistently externally. The frustration that simmers in the morning huddle shows up in the tone of the afternoon confirmation calls. The unresolved tension between the front desk and the clinical team surfaces in the handoff moments when patients transition from one part of the practice to another.

Awareness of internal team communication is not about creating a surveillance culture. It is about understanding that everything the team experiences together shapes everything the patient experiences — and that a practice cannot consistently communicate care externally while experiencing conflict internally.

The Revenue Gap Reality

Here is something that surprises almost every practice owner who goes through a genuine awareness process:

The revenue gaps in most practices are not where anyone expected to find them.

They are not primarily in the marketing budget or the fee schedule or the insurance mix. They are in the conversations. The phone calls that did not convert. The treatment plans that were presented once and never followed up on. The overdue hygiene patients who received a reminder postcard instead of a warm personal call. The new patient who scheduled, cancelled once, and was never contacted again.

These gaps are invisible until you measure them. And most practices do not measure them because they do not know they exist.

Consider the unscheduled treatment gap alone.

In the average dental practice at any given time there is a significant dollar amount of diagnosed but unscheduled treatment sitting in the patient database. Treatment that the dentist has already recommended. Treatment that the patient has already been told they need. Treatment that is not happening — not because the patient definitively refused, but because the follow-up conversation never happened, or happened in a way that did not invite the patient back in.

That number — the value of diagnosed but unscheduled treatment in your practice right now — is one of the most important numbers in your business. And in most practices nobody knows what it is.

Awareness makes it visible. And once it is visible it becomes impossible to ignore — and remarkably straightforward to address with the right language and the right follow-up system.

As John Maxwell puts it:

"The more seriously you take your growth, the more seriously your team will take theirs."

When leadership commits to the awareness process — when the practice owner or office manager genuinely engages with what the practice looks and sounds like from the outside — the team follows. The culture of honest self-assessment that awareness creates is itself a form of growth modeling. And growth modeled at the top of a practice spreads downward and outward with remarkable speed.

The Morning Huddle as an Awareness Tool

One of the most underutilized awareness opportunities in dentistry is the morning huddle.

In most practices the morning huddle — when it happens at all — is a logistical exercise. Who is coming in today. What procedures are scheduled. Any lab cases to check on. Done in seven minutes, often while someone is still eating breakfast.

That is scheduling coordination. It is not awareness.

A morning huddle designed around A.L.I.G.N.™ awareness principles does something different. It asks different questions. Not just *"who is coming in today"* but *"what does each patient coming in today need from us communicatively?"* Not just *"what procedures are scheduled"* but *"are there any patients on today's schedule with unscheduled treatment — and who is going to have that conversation, and how?"*

It surfaces opportunities that a purely logistical huddle misses entirely. The patient coming in for a cleaning who has been avoiding a crown recommendation for six months. The new patient whose intake form mentioned dental anxiety. The patient who called yesterday with a financial concern that the front desk handled but that the clinical team does not know about.

When the morning huddle becomes an awareness exercise — when it is used to deliberately prepare the team for the communication opportunities and challenges the day holds — it transforms from a logistical formality into one of the most powerful culture-building tools in the practice.

And it takes exactly the same amount of time.

Awareness Is Not Criticism

Before we close this chapter I want to address something that comes up consistently when practices begin the awareness process.

Awareness work can feel uncomfortable. Particularly for team members who have been doing their jobs with genuine dedication for years — and who discover, through the awareness process, that certain habitual phrases have been working against them without their knowledge.

The discomfort is understandable. Nobody enjoys discovering that something they have been doing confidently was quietly causing harm. The natural human response is defensiveness — and a leader who presents awareness findings in a critical or accusatory way will get exactly that response, shutting down the very openness that the awareness process requires.

Awareness in the A.L.I.G.N.™ framework is never about blame. It is never about catching people doing things wrong. It is about shining a light on patterns — organizational patterns, communication patterns, cultural patterns — so that the practice can make informed choices about what to keep and what to change.

John Maxwell addresses the leader's responsibility in this moment directly:

"A good leader is a person who takes a little more than his share of the blame and a little less than his share of the credit."

When awareness reveals a communication gap the leader's job is not to point at the team member who has been saying the wrong thing. It is to acknowledge that the practice — as a system — never gave that team member the tools to say the right thing. The gap is not personal. It is systemic. And systemic gaps require systemic solutions.

That is exactly what the remaining pillars of A.L.I.G.N.™ provide.

Awareness shows you where you are.

Language, Identity, Goals, and Navigation show you how to get where you want to be.

The Awareness Audit — Where to Start

If you are reading this and thinking *"I want to do this — but where do I actually begin?"* here is a simple starting framework.

Spend one week doing nothing but observing and listening. Do not change anything yet. Do not correct anything yet. Simply pay attention — with fresh eyes and genuine curiosity — to these five things:

One. How is the phone being answered — in tone, in language, and in outcome? Are calls converting to appointments? If not, at what point in the conversation does the momentum shift?

Two. How is treatment being presented — in the operatory, at the front desk, and in follow-up conversations? Is the language clinical and distancing or warm and educational?

Three. How are financial conversations being handled? Does money feel like a barrier in your practice or a bridge?

Four. How is the team communicating internally? Is the morning huddle a genuine preparation tool or a logistical formality?

Five. What does your patient database tell you about unscheduled treatment, overdue hygiene patients, and new patient conversion? What are the numbers — and when did you last look at them honestly?

Write down what you observe. Not to build a case against anyone. To build a picture of where the practice currently stands — clearly, specifically, and honestly.

That picture is your starting point.

And as John Maxwell reminds us — the starting point, honestly faced, is never something to fear:

"You don't have to be great to start, but you have to start to be great."

The awareness process is the start.

Everything that follows builds on it.

Chapter Takeaway

Awareness is the foundation of the A.L.I.G.N.™ system — and the starting point of every genuine practice transformation. Most dental practices have significant communication blind spots that are invisible from the inside and costly in ways that never show up clearly on a production report. Awareness work makes these blind spots visible — through honest observation of the phone experience, treatment presentation, financial conversations, team communication, and patient database realities. It is not about blame or criticism. It is about giving a practice the clear sight it needs to make informed, intentional changes. You cannot fix what you cannot see. Awareness gives you the sight.

What This Means for Your Practice

The recognition moment is real.

I have watched it happen hundreds of times — in team sessions, in phone audit reviews, in the quiet moment after a scheduling coordinator hears her own confirmation call played back and the room goes slightly still. The slight wince. The exhale. The quiet — oh.

That moment is not embarrassing. It is the beginning of everything.

Because the team member who genuinely sees what their words are doing — not because they were told but because they actually heard it and felt it — does not need to be managed into changing. They want to change. The motivation is immediate and personal and genuinely theirs.

That is the power of awareness over instruction. Instruction produces compliance. Awareness produces commitment.

-Here's What I Want You to Remember-

Pick one phone call this week and listen to it as if you are the patient. Not the practice owner. Not the office manager. The patient — who called with a real need, who found your practice, who worked up the courage to make the call.

What did they experience? Write it down. That note is the beginning of your Awareness work. And everything that follows in this book gets stronger the more honestly you answer that question.

Chapter 6
L is for Language

The Right Words at the Right Moment Change Everything

"Words are free. It's how you use them that may cost you." — John Maxwell

There is a small but extraordinary experiment you can conduct right now — without leaving your chair, without spending a dollar, and without involving a single member of your team.

Read these two sentences and pay attention to how each one makes you feel:

"You owe $250 today."

"Your portion for today's visit is $250."

Same number. Same financial reality. Same checkout moment in the same dental practice.

Different world.

The first sentence positions the practice as a creditor and the patient as a debtor. It carries the subtle but unmistakable weight of obligation — of something owed, something past due, something that has already created a deficit that must now be settled. It is transactional in the least flattering sense of that word.

The second sentence positions the practice as a partner. The word "portion" implies that the cost is shared — that the practice, the insurance, and the patient are all contributing to something together. The phrase "today's visit" grounds the conversation in the value of what just happened rather than the burden of what must now be paid. It is still a request for $250. But it feels entirely different.

That feeling is not accidental. It is not manipulation. It is the natural result of choosing words with intention — of understanding that language does not just convey information. It creates experience. And the experience a patient has in your practice is shaped, moment by moment, word by word, by the language your team chooses in every single interaction.

This chapter is about those choices.

"The tongue has no bones, but is strong enough to break a heart. So be careful with your words." — attributed to various sources, cited frequently by John Maxwell

Why Language Is the Highest-Leverage Skill in Your Practice

Of all the investments a dental practice can make — technology, marketing, facility upgrades, additional services — none produces a faster, more measurable, more sustainable return than intentional language training.

Here is why.

Technology improves one aspect of the clinical experience. Marketing attracts new patients to the door. Facility upgrades enhance the physical environment. All of these are valuable. None of them determine what happens in the conversation.

Language determines what happens in the conversation. And the conversation — the sum total of every word spoken between your team and your patients from the first phone call to the final goodbye — is where trust is built or broken, where treatment is accepted or declined, where patients decide to stay or quietly drift away.

Language is present in every single patient interaction. It costs nothing to change. It can be improved immediately. And its impact compounds across every category of practice performance simultaneously — new patient conversion, case acceptance, retention, reactivation, referrals, and team culture — all at once.

No piece of technology does that. No marketing campaign does that. No office renovation does that.

Only language does that.

John Maxwell writes:

"The most important thing in communication is hearing what isn't said."

And I would add — the most powerful thing in communication is being intentional about what is said. Because in a dental practice the words that are spoken — and the words that are chosen instead of other words — shape the entire patient relationship from beginning to end.

The Neuroscience of Trust

You do not need a degree in neuroscience to understand why certain words work and others do not. But it helps to know that the research fully supports what experienced communicators have always known intuitively.

When a person hears language that feels threatening, dismissive, or judgmental — even subtly — the brain's threat response activates. Cortisol rises. Defensiveness increases. The capacity for open, receptive listening narrows. The person in front of you is still physically present — but emotionally they have already started to leave.

This is not a character flaw. It is basic human neurology. And it happens in dental practices dozens of times a day — triggered not by dramatic confrontations but by small, seemingly innocuous phrases that carry an unconscious emotional charge.

"You need to floss more." — triggers shame. *"Your insurance doesn't cover that."* — triggers abandonment. *"We're running behind."* — triggers frustration. *"You should've called sooner."* — triggers guilt. *"That's how long it takes."* — triggers dismissal.

None of these phrases are delivered with malicious intent. All of them activate the threat response in the patient receiving them. And a patient in a threat response does not accept treatment, does not reschedule, does not refer their friends, and does not leave a five-star review.

Now consider the neurological effect of language that feels warm, collaborative, and solution-focused.

When a person hears language that validates their experience, acknowledges their concern, and offers a path forward — the brain's reward circuitry activates. Oxytocin — the neurochemical of trust and connection — increases. Openness expands. The capacity to hear, consider, and respond positively grows.

"Let's review techniques that can help improve your home care results." — invites collaboration. *"Your insurance provides an estimated contribution toward your treatment."* — maintains partnership. *"Thank you for your patience — we appreciate your understanding today."* — disarms frustration. *"Thank you for letting us know. Let's find another time to continue your care."* — preserves relationship. *"We reserve this*

time so the doctor can provide thorough, uninterrupted care." — reframes value.

Same situations. Completely different neurological experience for the patient.

This is not soft science. This is the hard reality of how human beings process language — and why the words your team chooses matter far more than most practices have ever been taught.

The Positive Framing Principle

At the heart of A.L.I.G.N.™ language training is a principle so simple it almost sounds too simple to be transformative:

Lead with what you can do. Not what you cannot.

This is the positive framing principle. And it is violated in dental practices hundreds of times every single day — not out of negativity, but out of habit.

"We can't give fees over the phone." "We don't have anything available until next month." "We're not in network with your insurance." "We can't squeeze you in today." "You're not eligible for that yet."

Every one of these responses leads with a negative — a can't, a don't, a not, a won't. And every one of them, regardless of what follows, creates an immediate experience of limitation for the patient.

The positive framing principle does not ask you to be dishonest. It does not ask you to pretend that limitations do not exist. It asks you to lead with the possibility rather than the restriction — to put what you can do at the front of the sentence and let what you cannot do follow if it needs to be mentioned at all.

"I'd be happy to help you understand what to expect and reserve time for your visit." "Our most requested times reserve quickly — let's review the best options together." "We'll help you maximize any available benefits." "Let's find the soonest time available to get you taken care of." "Your insurance plan has timing guidelines for coverage."

The information is essentially the same. The experience is entirely different. And in patient communication the experience is everything.

Brené Brown captures the underlying principle beautifully:

"Vulnerability is the birthplace of innovation, creativity and change."

Positive framing is connection language. It keeps the door open. It keeps the patient in the conversation. It signals — in every word — that the practice is on their side.

Language Across Every Touchpoint

One of the things that makes A.L.I.G.N.™ language training different from generic communication coaching is its specificity. It does not traffic in vague principles like *"be more empathetic"* or *"use positive language."* It addresses the specific conversations that happen in specific moments across the entire patient journey — and gives the team the exact language for each one.

Let us walk through the patient journey and look at what intentional language actually looks like at each touchpoint.

The First Phone Call

The first phone call is the most consequential conversation in the patient relationship — because it determines whether there is a patient relationship at all.

A new patient calling a dental practice for the first time is almost always experiencing some degree of anxiety. They may be anxious about dental care itself. They may be anxious about cost. They may be anxious about being judged for how long it has been since their last visit. They are reaching out despite that anxiety — which means the very first words they hear need to reward that courage rather than confirm their fears.

The single most important language principle for the first phone call is this:

Make the patient feel like the call was expected and the answer is yes.

Not yes to everything. Not yes to unreasonable requests. But yes to the underlying emotional need of the call — which is almost always some version of *"is there a place for me here?"*

"I'd be happy to help you with that." "We'd love to get you scheduled." "Let's find a time that works perfectly for you."

These phrases do not commit the practice to anything it cannot deliver. They create an experience of welcome — of being wanted — that sets the entire patient relationship on the right foundation.

Compare that to the experience of hearing *"we can't give fees over the phone"* or *"let me put you on hold"* as the first response to a new patient's first question. The foundation those phrases build is one of barriers and inconvenience — and foundations, once laid, are very difficult to change.

The Insurance Conversation

Few moments in the dental practice create more patient anxiety — or more communication landmines — than the insurance conversation.

Insurance is confusing. It is inconsistent. It creates expectations that do not always match reality. And when those expectations are not met, patients often feel cheated — not necessarily by the insurance company but by the practice that they feel did not adequately prepare them.

The language of insurance in most dental practices defaults to the passive — *"insurance won't cover that," "your insurance doesn't include that,"* as though the practice is simply a messenger for the insurance company's decisions and bears no responsibility for helping the patient navigate them.

A.L.I.G.N.™ insurance language does something different. It positions the practice as the patient's advocate — someone who is working on their behalf to maximize whatever benefits are available, regardless of the limitations.

"Your insurance provides an estimated contribution toward your treatment." — not *"your insurance doesn't cover that."*

"Your plan reimburses based on an alternative benefit allowance." — not *"insurance downgraded it."*

"We'll help you maximize any available out-of-network benefits." — not *"we don't take your insurance."*

"You've utilized most of your annual benefits." — not *"you're maxed out."*

The shift in each case is the same. From passive messenger to active advocate. From limitation to partnership. From the patient feeling alone in a confusing system to feeling supported by a practice that is in their corner.

That feeling of being supported — particularly around something as anxiety-inducing as insurance and money — is one of the most powerful loyalty-builders available to any dental practice. And it costs nothing to create. It requires only the right words.

The Financial Conversation

Money is the conversation most dental team members dread. And that dread — however well-concealed — communicates itself to the patient.

The patient picks up on the slight tension in the coordinator's voice when a large treatment estimate is presented. They notice the barely perceptible shift from warmth to efficiency when the conversation turns to payment. They feel the unspoken discomfort that surrounds financial discussions in most dental practices — and they interpret it, unconsciously, as a signal that they are being asked for something the practice is not entirely comfortable asking for.

That interpretation is devastating to case acceptance.

A.L.I.G.N.™ financial language is built on a single foundational principle:

Talk about money the way you talk about health. With confidence, clarity, and genuine care.

The practice is not asking for a favor when it collects payment. It is completing a transaction that makes exceptional care sustainable. There is nothing to be apologetic or uncomfortable about. And when the language reflects that confidence — when the team presents financial information with the same calm clarity they bring to clinical information — the patient's anxiety about money drops measurably.

"This treatment is an investment in protecting your long-term oral health." — not *"it's expensive, I know."*

"We have flexible options that may help make treatment more comfortable financially." — not *"you'll need to pay in full."*

"To reserve this dedicated treatment time we collect a scheduling deposit." — not *"we require money upfront."*

"We wanted to help you bring your account current and discuss available options." — not *"your account is delinquent."*

In every case the language shift moves the conversation from confrontation to collaboration. From the practice and the patient facing each other across a financial divide to standing side by side, looking together at the options available to move forward.

Dale Carnegie identified the underlying principle nearly a century ago — and it has lost none of its truth:

"The only way to get the best of an argument is to avoid it."

Financial language that creates defensiveness creates an argument — even when no voices are raised and no one storms out. The patient simply says they will think about it. And thinking about it, in the context of a conversation that felt uncomfortable, almost always means saying no quietly and never coming back.

Financial language that creates partnership creates conversation. And conversation creates decisions. And decisions — made in an environment of trust and support — far more often result in yes.

The Treatment Presentation

Treatment presentation is where the Language pillar of A.L.I.G.N.™ has perhaps its most direct and measurable impact — because the gap between how most practices present treatment and how patients need to receive it is enormous.

Most treatment presentations are clinically accurate and emotionally tone-deaf.

The dentist — trained for years in the science of oral health, fluent in the language of pathology and procedure — presents treatment in the language they know best. Clinical language. Diagnostic language. The language of conditions and consequences and procedural solutions.

"You have a cracked cusp on tooth number fourteen. If we don't address it with a crown the crack could propagate to the root and you could lose the tooth."

Every word of that sentence is accurate. Every word of it activates the patient's threat response. The word *"crack"* triggers alarm. *"Propagate"* sounds catastrophic. *"Lose the tooth"* lands like a verdict.

The patient, flooded with anxiety, retreats into their most protective response:

"Can I think about it?"

What they are really saying is: *"I need to escape this feeling."*

Now consider the same clinical reality presented through A.L.I.G.N.™ language principles:

"We found some stress on tooth number fourteen — the kind that develops over time with normal biting and chewing. What we'd like to do is place a crown to strengthen and protect it before any further stress develops. Our goal is always to protect what you have for as long as possible."

Same tooth. Same condition. Same recommended treatment.

But this time the patient hears that something normal happened — *"stress that develops over time"* — not that something is catastrophically wrong. They hear that the practice wants to *protect* something they value — not that they are facing a loss. They hear *"our goal"* — which signals partnership rather than prescription.

And far more often they say yes.

John Maxwell writes:

"Communication is not just words. It is the tone, intent, and emotion behind the words that determines whether people truly hear you."

Treatment presentation is the moment in the dental practice where tone, intent, and emotion matter most — because the patient is at their most vulnerable, their most anxious, and their most receptive to either reassurance or alarm.

A.L.I.G.N.™ language gives every clinician — doctor and hygienist alike — the framework to present treatment in a way that informs without alarming, recommends without pressuring, and invites a yes rather than triggering a retreat.

The Reactivation Call

Of all the communication moments in a dental practice the reactivation call may be the one most consistently handled in a way that produces the opposite of the intended result.

The intention is to bring an overdue patient back in. The language used to do it almost universally produces shame, guilt, and defensiveness — the three emotions least likely to result in a scheduled appointment.

"You're overdue for your cleaning." "You haven't been in since 2022." "You still haven't scheduled that treatment we recommended." "You need to get this taken care of."

Every one of these openings positions the patient as someone who has done something wrong. And people who feel accused do not respond with enthusiasm. They respond with avoidance.

The patient who has not been in for two years already knows they have not been in for two years. They do not need to be informed of their delinquency. They need to be given a reason to come back that feels welcoming rather than punitive.

"We wanted to reach out and help you continue protecting your oral health." "We've been thinking about you and wanted to see how you're doing." "We wanted to follow up and see if you had any questions about your recommended treatment." "We're here to help when you feel ready to move forward."

The difference is not just tonal. It is philosophical. These phrases are not pretending the gap in care did not happen. They are simply choosing not to lead with it — because leading with the gap produces defensiveness and leading with care produces connection.

And connection — not guilt — is what brings patients back.

The Language of Leadership

Language in the A.L.I.G.N.™ framework does not apply only to patient communication. It applies equally to how leaders communicate with their teams — because the internal language of a practice is the foundation on which the external language is built.

A leader who says *"we have holes in the schedule"* trains the team to think about open appointments as problems — deficits to be filled, failures to be explained. A leader who says *"we have opportunities to serve additional patients today"* trains the team to think about open appointments as possibilities — chances to help someone who needs care.

That is not spin. That is culture. And culture is built one sentence at a time — by the words leaders choose in morning huddles, in team meetings, in the hallway conversations that nobody thinks of as leadership moments but that are, in fact, the most powerful leadership moments of all.

John Maxwell is emphatic on this point:

"A leader's words carry extra weight. Choose them accordingly."

When a practice owner says *"you dropped the ball"* to a team member who missed a responsibility, that phrase does not just describe what happened. It defines the team member — as someone who drops balls, who fails, who is not reliable. The defensiveness it creates closes the door to the very growth conversation that was needed.

"Let's review what happened and how we can improve moving forward" opens that door. Same situation. Completely different outcome.

The leader who chooses language intentionally — in every interaction, with every team member, in every situation — creates a team that mirrors that intentionality with every patient. Because teams do not communicate above the level their leaders model.

Language flows downhill. Make sure what is flowing is something worth spreading.

The Team Language Audit

One of the most powerful exercises in A.L.I.G.N.™ language training is what I call the Team Language Audit — and it is something every practice can do this week without any external help.

Gather your team. Ask each person to write down — honestly and without judgment — the three phrases they use most often in difficult patient interactions. The go-to responses. The phrases that come out automatically when a patient asks about cost, pushes back on treatment, calls to cancel, or expresses frustration.

Then read them aloud together.

What you will discover — almost without exception — is that the most commonly used phrases are the ones that create the most barriers. Not because the team is negative or uncaring. Because those phrases were inherited, never examined, and repeated until they became invisible habits.

Once they are visible they can be changed.

This is the language audit. It is uncomfortable for about fifteen minutes and transformative for years afterward.

As John Maxwell writes:

"Change is very difficult. But once a decision is made, change becomes much easier. The pain of change is temporary, but the pain of remaining the same can last a lifetime."

The language habits that are costing your practice patients, production, and culture right now will not change on their own. They will not improve because of good intentions or general awareness. They will change when your team sees them clearly, understands why they need to change, and is given the specific replacement language to practice until the new habits become as automatic as the old ones were.

That is what A.L.I.G.N.™ Language training does.

It replaces the invisible habits that hurt with intentional habits that heal.

A Final Thought on Language

I want to close this chapter with something that goes deeper than technique.

The reason language matters so profoundly in a dental practice is not ultimately about case acceptance rates or new patient conversion numbers or reactivation success percentages — though all of those improve when the language improves.

The reason language matters is because every patient who calls your practice or sits in your chair is a human being navigating something that makes them vulnerable. They may be in pain. They may be afraid. They may be embarrassed about the state of their oral health. They may be anxious about money. They may have had a bad experience somewhere else that makes them reluctant to trust again.

And in that vulnerability they are paying attention — consciously or not — to every signal your team sends about whether this is a safe place to be.

Your language is that signal.

Every word your team speaks is either telling that patient *"you are safe here, you are valued here, we are on your side"* — or it is telling them something else.

Maya Angelou said it in a way that no one has ever said it better:

"I've learned that whenever I decide something with an open heart, I usually make the right decision."

The language of A.L.I.G.N.™ is built to make people feel something specific.

Seen. Heard. Supported. Valued.

And people who feel that way in your practice do not just become patients.

They become advocates. They become loyalists. They become the people who send their families to you, who defend you in online reviews, who stay with you through staff changes and office moves and the inevitable imperfections of any human endeavor.

They become the foundation of a practice that does not just survive.

It thrives.

Chapter Takeaway

Language is the highest-leverage skill in any dental practice — present in every patient interaction, immediately changeable, and with an impact that compounds across every category of practice performance simultaneously. The A.L.I.G.N.™ Language pillar is built on three core principles: positive framing leads with what you can do rather than what you cannot; empathetic language responds to the emotional reality of the patient, not just the clinical or administrative reality; and intentional language is specific to each touchpoint — the phone call, the insurance conversation, the financial discussion, the treatment presentation, the reactivation call, and the internal team communication that underlies all of them. Language does not just convey information. It creates experience. And the experience your patients have in your practice — shaped word by word, moment by moment — determines everything.

What This Means for Your Practice

Here is the thing about language that took me years to fully appreciate.

The words are not the hard part.

The hard part is understanding why certain words work and others do not — at a level deep enough that the knowledge becomes instinctive rather than effortful. Deep enough that the right phrase comes naturally under pressure, in the difficult conversation, on the busy Tuesday morning when everything is happening at once and there is no time to think about what to say next.

That depth of understanding is what the Language pillar builds. Not a list of phrases to memorize. A genuine comprehension of the mechanism — why warmth lands, why limitation language triggers resistance, why the assumptive confirmation call reduces cancellations in a way the questioning one never will.

When your team understands the why the what takes care of itself.

-Here's What I Want You to Remember-

Go back to the Instead Of contrasts in this chapter and pick the one that made you wince most in recognition. The one where you thought — we say that. We say that every single day.

Start there. Practice that one replacement this week. Out loud. In the morning huddle. With real feedback from real colleagues. Just one. Because one language change practiced consistently produces more lasting improvement than ten language changes practiced occasionally.

Start with the one that matters most.

Chapter 7

I is for Identity

Who Your Practice IS Determines How Your Practice Speaks

"Everything rises and falls on leadership." — John Maxwell

There is a question I ask every practice owner I work with — usually within the first hour of our first conversation together. It is not a question about production numbers or case acceptance rates or new patient flow. It is not a question about systems or scheduling or insurance mix.

It is this:

"How do your patients describe your practice when you are not in the room?"

The question almost always produces a pause.

Not because the practice owner does not care about the answer. Because they realize — often for the first time — that they do not actually know it.

They know how they want patients to describe the practice. They know the words they would choose if they were writing the description themselves. Warm. Professional. State-of-the-art. Caring. The kind of place where you actually feel comfortable.

But what patients say when the practice owner is not listening — in the car on the way home, at the dinner table that night, to the colleague who mentions they are looking for a new dentist — that is a different question entirely. And the gap between how a practice wants to be perceived and how it is actually experienced by the people who walk through its doors is one of the most important and most consistently unexamined gaps in dentistry.

That gap is an identity gap.

And closing it — building a practice identity so clear, so consistent, and so genuinely lived that what patients say in the car matches what the practice owner hoped they would say — is the work of the Identity pillar of A.L.I.G.N.™

"Leadership is influence — nothing more, nothing less." — John Maxwell

What Identity Actually Means

When most people hear the word identity in a business context they think of branding. Logo. Color palette. Tagline. The visual language that a practice presents to the world through its website, its signage, and its marketing materials.

That is not what we are talking about here.

Brand is what a practice says it is. Identity is what a practice actually is — in the daily reality of every patient interaction, every team conversation, every leadership decision, and every word spoken in every moment when nobody is watching and no marketing consultant is taking notes.

Brand can be designed in an afternoon. Identity is built over years — through the accumulation of thousands of small choices about how to treat people, how to respond to difficulty, how to lead under pressure, and how to communicate when it would be easier not to.

And here is the truth that makes identity so powerful — and so consequential:

Patients cannot always articulate your brand. But they feel your identity every single time they interact with your practice. And that feeling — reliable, consistent, and unmistakably yours — is what creates loyalty that no competitor can replicate and no marketing budget can manufacture.

John Maxwell writes:

"Image is what people think we are. Integrity is what we really are."

Identity, in the A.L.I.G.N.™ framework, is integrity made visible. It is the alignment between what a practice claims to be and what it actually does — in every conversation, at every touchpoint, with every patient and every team member, every single day.

The Leader Sets the Temperature

Here is the most important thing I have learned in over 38 years of working inside dental practices:

The emotional temperature of a practice is set by its leader.

Not by the office manager. Not by the most senior team member. Not by the patient experience consultant or the practice management software or the carefully worded mission statement hanging in the reception area.

By the leader.

Specifically — by the words the leader uses, the tone the leader carries, and the behavior the leader models in every interaction with the team.

This is not a soft observation. It is a measurable, observable, entirely predictable pattern that plays out with remarkable consistency across practices of every size, every specialty, and every market. The practices that communicate warmly and consistently with patients almost always have a leader who communicates warmly and consistently with the team. The practices where financial conversations feel pressured and clinical presentations feel alarming almost always have a leader whose own communication style — however unintentionally — models pressure and alarm.

Teams do not communicate above the level their leaders model.

Read that again.

Teams do not communicate above the level their leaders model.

If the dentist says *"we're booked"* when the schedule is full, the front desk coordinator says *"we're booked"* when the schedule is full. If the dentist presents treatment with urgency and fear — *"you really don't want to let this go"* — the team presents treatment with urgency and fear. If the dentist handles a difficult team conversation with blame and frustration, the team handles difficult patient conversations with defensiveness and avoidance.

The reverse is equally true. And equally powerful.

When a leader communicates with intentional warmth, the team communicates with intentional warmth. When a leader models solution-focused language in the morning huddle, the team uses solution-focused language with patients. When a leader handles a mistake with coaching curiosity rather than criticism, the team handles patient concerns with the same generous spirit.

John Maxwell has written about this dynamic more extensively than almost anyone:

"The speed of the leader is the speed of the gang."

In a dental practice the language of the leader is the language of the practice. Full stop. Which means that Identity work — genuine, lasting practice identity work — must begin with the leader. Not with the front desk team. Not with the scheduling coordinator or the hygienist or the dental assistant. With the person whose words and tone and behavior establish the daily standard that everyone else in the practice either rises to or defaults from.

That person is you.

The Practice Identity Audit

How do you know what your practice identity actually is — as opposed to what you intend it to be?

You listen. Specifically, you listen for three things.

What your team says when they do not know you are listening.

Not surveillance. Awareness. The conversation at the front desk between patient check-ins. The tone of the confirmation calls made when the schedule gets tight. The way a team member describes the practice to a new patient who asks how long they have worked there. The language used in the morning huddle when the day looks difficult.

These unscripted moments are the truest expression of your practice identity — because they happen without the self-consciousness that comes from knowing the leader is paying attention. They reveal the culture that has actually taken root, as opposed to the culture that was intended.

What your patients say in their reviews — and what they do not say.

Online reviews are a remarkably honest identity audit. Patients who feel genuinely cared for say so — in specific, emotional language that goes well beyond *"great dentist, clean office."* They say things like *"I actually looked forward to my appointment"* and *"they made me feel like a person, not a patient"* and *"I've recommended them to everyone I know."*

Patients who feel processed rather than cared for either say nothing — they simply do not leave a review — or they leave reviews that praise the clinical quality while conspicuously omitting any mention of how the practice made them feel.

Read your reviews not for the star rating but for the emotional language. What feeling do patients describe? Is it the feeling you intended to create?

What your team members say when they leave.

Exit interviews — when practices conduct them honestly — are one of the most revealing identity audits available. Team members who leave dental practices almost never cite clinical disagreements or compensation alone as their primary reason. They cite culture. They describe feeling like a number. Feeling pressured to perform without being given the tools to perform well. Feeling that the values the practice claimed to hold were not the values it actually practiced.

Every exit interview is a message from your identity to your intentions.

Are you receiving it?

Leadership Identity — The Inner Work

There is a dimension of Identity work in A.L.I.G.N.™ that goes deeper than communication style and team culture. It is the inner work of leadership identity — the question of how the practice owner sees themselves as a leader, and whether that self-perception aligns with the leadership the practice actually needs.

Most dentists did not choose their career because they wanted to be leaders. They chose it because they wanted to help people — to use their hands and their minds and their clinical skill to improve someone's health and quality of life. Leadership was not part of the description. It came with the building.

And for many practice owners the transition from clinician to leader — from the person doing the work to the person responsible for everyone doing the work — is one that never fully happens. They remain clinicians who happen to own a practice rather than leaders who happen to practice dentistry.

The difference is not semantic. It is everything.

A clinician who happens to own a practice makes decisions based on clinical logic — what is best for this patient in this chair right now. A leader who happens to practice dentistry makes decisions based on cultural logic — what is best for this practice, this team, and the hundreds of patients whose experience depends on how well that team is led.

A clinician who owns a practice communicates reactively — responding to problems as they arise, dealing with team issues when they become unavoidable, addressing communication gaps when they become crises. A leader who practices dentistry communicates proactively — setting the standard before problems arise, building the culture before the crisis, modeling the language before the team needs it.

John Maxwell makes the distinction with characteristic directness:

"The difference between a boss and a leader: a boss says 'Go!' — a leader says 'Let's go!'"

Identity work invites every practice owner to ask — honestly and without defensiveness — which one am I? Not which one do I want to be. Which one am I actually being, today, in this practice, with this team?

That question is not comfortable. It is necessary. Because the answer determines everything about the practice's capacity to grow — and to sustain that growth over time.

Building a Team Identity

Leadership identity is the foundation. Team identity is the structure built on it.

Team identity in the A.L.I.G.N.™ framework is the shared sense of who we are and how we do things here that every member of the team carries with them into every patient interaction. It is what makes the practice feel consistent to patients regardless of which team member they speak with. It is what makes a new hire feel the culture of the practice within their first week — not because anyone sat them down and recited the mission statement, but because the culture is so clearly lived by everyone around them that it is impossible not to absorb it.

Building team identity requires three things.

A clearly articulated standard.

Not a mission statement. A standard — a specific, behavioral description of how this practice communicates, treats people, and shows up in every interaction. Not *"we provide exceptional patient care"* — which is what every practice says and means nothing. But *"in this practice we lead every patient interaction with warmth and solutions, we never make a patient feel like a burden, and we always leave a person feeling better for having spoken with us."*

That is a standard. It is specific enough to guide behavior. It is clear enough to hold people accountable to. And it is meaningful enough that team members who share those values will be proud to uphold it.

Consistent modeling from leadership.

A standard that is articulated but not modeled is a sign on the wall. A standard that is modeled — lived out loud, every day, by the person with the most influence in the practice — is a culture.

The practice owner who wants the front desk team to greet every patient warmly must greet every team member warmly. The leader who wants the hygienist to respond to patient fear with empathy must respond to team member mistakes with empathy. The culture you want your patients to experience is the culture you must create for your team.

As John Maxwell writes:

"People do what people see."

Show them what you want. Then show them again. And again. Until it becomes the air the practice breathes.

Intentional onboarding.

Team identity is most vulnerable at the point of new hire onboarding — because new team members arrive as blank slates, ready to absorb whatever culture they find. In practices with strong identity those new hires are immersed in the culture deliberately and immediately — through structured conversations about how the practice communicates, through guided observation of experienced team members, through clear articulation of the standard and why it matters.

In practices without intentional onboarding new team members learn the culture by observation alone — which means they absorb both its strengths and its blind spots in equal measure. The inherited habits that the awareness process was designed to uncover get passed along to the next generation of team members before anyone has had a chance to examine them.

Intentional onboarding is identity protection. It ensures that the culture grows forward rather than replicating its own blind spots with every new hire.

When Identity and Language Align

There is a moment in every practice coaching engagement that I consider the true turning point — the moment when I know that the work is going to stick.

It is not when the production numbers improve. It is not when the case acceptance rate climbs or the reactivation calls start working or the new patient reviews start glowing with emotional language.

It is the moment when a team member uses intentional, trust-building, patient-centered language — not because they were reminded to, not because the script said to, not because the practice owner was watching —

But because it was simply who they are now.

Because the language and the identity have aligned.

Because the way they communicate with patients is no longer a technique they are performing. It is an expression of something they genuinely believe about the value of their work and the people they serve.

That moment — quiet, unremarkable from the outside, and profoundly significant from the inside — is what practice identity transformation actually looks and feels like.

It does not announce itself. It simply shows up one day in the way a scheduling coordinator handles a difficult phone call. In the way a hygienist responds to a patient's expressed fear. In the way a dentist presents a treatment recommendation — not as a clinical directive but as a genuine act of care for someone they value.

John Maxwell describes this state with words that have stayed with me since the first time I read them:

"The whole of life is about one thing — becoming who you were meant to be."

For a dental practice the equivalent truth is this:

The whole of practice development is about one thing — becoming the practice you were always capable of being.

Identity work is how you get there.

Not through marketing. Not through production targets. Not through scripted techniques or weekend retreats or the latest practice management software.

Through the daily, intentional, leadership-modeled, team-lived reality of who you choose to be — in every word, every interaction, every moment of connection with the people who trust you with their health.

That is identity.

And when it is genuine — when it is lived rather than performed — patients feel it the moment they walk through the door.

They feel it so clearly and so unmistakably that they cannot imagine going anywhere else.

Chapter Takeaway

Identity is the pillar of A.L.I.G.N.™ that determines whether everything else lasts. It operates on two levels — leadership identity and practice identity — and both are shaped by one primary force: the daily language, tone, and behavior of the person at the top. Teams mirror their leaders. Practices become what their leaders consistently model. The work of Identity in A.L.I.G.N.™ is the work of closing the gap between the practice a leader intends to lead and the practice that patients actually experience — through honest self-assessment, a clearly articulated and consistently modeled team standard, and the intentional onboarding that protects the culture as the practice grows. When language and identity align — when the words team members use are not a performance but an expression of who they genuinely are — the practice stops being a place patients visit and becomes a place patients belong.

What This Means for Your Practice

The identity question is the one I save for the right moment in every coaching engagement.

Not because it is complicated. Because it requires a specific kind of honesty that most people need time to arrive at. The dentist who has spent twenty years defining themselves entirely through clinical excellence. The front desk coordinator who has spent six years seeing herself as someone who answers phones and manages schedules rather than as the first human connection a new patient makes with a practice that genuinely cares for them.

That redefinition — from function to relationship, from role to genuine contribution — does not happen through instruction. It happens through the specific, honest, facilitated conversation that invites each person to see themselves more completely.

I have watched that conversation change people. Not their skills. Them. The way they carry themselves. The way they answer the phone. The way they walk past a patient in the waiting room and choose — consciously, specifically — to acknowledge them rather than look at a screen.

-Here's What I Want You to Remember-

Ask your team this question in your next morning huddle. Not as an exercise. As a genuine question that deserves a genuine answer.

Who are we to our patients? Not what do we do. Who are we.

Listen to what they say. Because the answer to that question — specific, honest, and owned by the team rather than handed to them — is the foundation of everything the Identity pillar builds.

Chapter 8

G is for Goals

Vague Goals Produce Vague Results

"A dream is just a dream. A goal is a dream with a plan and a deadline."
— John Maxwell

Let me tell you about two dental practices.

Both are in the same city. Both have been open for roughly the same number of years. Both have dentists of comparable skill and teams of comparable size. Both attended the same study club last year where a speaker talked passionately about the importance of communication in practice growth. Both left that evening feeling inspired and motivated to make changes.

Six months later one practice has measurably improved its new patient conversion rate, reduced its cancellation rate, and increased case acceptance by eleven percentage points. The team talks about communication in the morning huddle. The office manager tracks specific metrics weekly. The dentist reviews progress with the team monthly and celebrates wins publicly.

The other practice is essentially where it was six months ago. The inspiration from the study club evening faded within two weeks. Nobody tracks communication metrics because nobody established any. The team remembers the speaker was good but cannot recall specifically what was supposed to change. Things are fine. Not worse. Just — fine.

The difference between these two practices is not motivation. Both were motivated.

The difference is not intention. Both intended to improve.

The difference is goals. Specific, measurable, accountable, tracked, and celebrated goals — versus the vague aspiration to do better that lives in the space between inspiration and implementation and produces nothing.

This chapter is about closing that space.

"Setting goals is the first step in turning the invisible into the visible." — Tony Robbins, cited frequently alongside John Maxwell in leadership contexts

Why Dental Practices Avoid Measurable Goals

Before we talk about how to set the right goals let us talk honestly about why most practices avoid setting them in the first place.

It is not laziness. It is not indifference. It is something more understandable and more human than either of those explanations.

It is the fear of accountability.

A vague goal — *"we want to improve our patient communication"* — carries no risk. It cannot be failed. It cannot be measured against and found wanting. It exists in a comfortable cloud of good intention that never has to confront the discomfort of a number that did not move in the right direction.

A specific goal — *"we will increase our new patient phone conversion rate from 58 percent to 72 percent over the next ninety days"* — is an entirely different proposition. It is visible. It is trackable. It will either be achieved or it will not. And if it is not achieved the practice will have to look honestly at why — which requires exactly the kind of self-examination that most people, most teams, and most organizations would prefer to avoid.

This avoidance is entirely human. And it is entirely costly.

Because here is what a specific, measurable goal does that a vague aspiration cannot:

It creates a feedback loop.

Without measurement there is no feedback. Without feedback there is no learning. Without learning there is no improvement. Without improvement there is no growth. The entire chain of practice development depends on the willingness to set goals specific enough to be measured — and to face the results of that measurement honestly, whether they are encouraging or uncomfortable.

John Maxwell addresses this directly:

"You cannot improve what you do not measure. And you cannot measure what you do not define."

Define the goal. Measure the progress. Improve based on what you learn. That is the entire logic of the Goals pillar of A.L.I.G.N.™ — and it is simpler in concept and more powerful in practice than most dental teams have ever been given the opportunity to discover.

The Right Goals for a Communication-Focused Practice

Here is where most practice goal-setting goes wrong — even in practices that do set specific, measurable targets.

The goals are almost exclusively financial.

Monthly production. Collections percentage. Revenue per hour. Cost per new patient acquisition. These are real numbers that matter genuinely to the health of the practice. But they are outcome metrics — they tell you what the practice produced, not why it produced it or how to produce more of it.

Communication metrics are leading indicators. They tell you not what already happened but what is about to happen — because the quality of the conversations happening today determines the production numbers that show up next month.

A practice that tracks its new patient phone conversion rate knows — in real time — whether the language training is working before it shows up in the monthly production report. A practice that tracks case acceptance by provider knows which team members need additional language coaching before the annual numbers reveal a pattern that has been building for twelve months. A practice that tracks reactivation success rates knows whether the outreach language is creating appointments or creating avoidance — and can adjust immediately rather than in the next annual review.

Communication metrics give practices something financial metrics alone cannot provide:

The ability to intervene early.

Before the problem becomes a trend. Before the trend becomes a crisis. Before the crisis becomes the reason someone calls a practice management consultant in a panic at the end of a difficult quarter.

In the A.L.I.G.N.™ framework the most important communication metrics for a dental practice to track fall into five categories.

The Five Communication Metrics That Matter Most

One — New Patient Phone Conversion Rate

Of every ten people who call your practice as a potential new patient how many schedule an appointment?

This is the single most revealing metric in the practice — because it measures the effectiveness of the first and most consequential communication touchpoint. Every percentage point of improvement in this number represents real patients who are now in your practice rather than the one down the street.

Industry benchmarks suggest that a well-trained front desk team should convert between 70 and 85 percent of qualified new patient inquiries into scheduled appointments. Many practices are converting considerably less without knowing it — because they have never measured it.

Start measuring it. Today. The number you find will be one of the most motivating discoveries your team makes.

Two — Case Acceptance Rate

Of the treatment diagnosed and presented in your practice how much of it is being accepted and scheduled?

This metric tells the story of how effectively the clinical team — doctors and hygienists — is communicating the value and necessity of recommended care. It should be tracked overall and by individual provider — not to create competition or shame, but to identify where language coaching is most needed and to measure the impact of that coaching over time.

A case acceptance rate significantly below 75 percent is almost always a communication story, not a clinical one. The treatment is appropriate. The recommendation is sound. Something in the presentation is creating resistance — and that something can be identified and addressed with the right language framework.

Three — Cancellation and No-Show Rate

What percentage of scheduled appointments are being cancelled — and of those cancellations how many are being successfully rescheduled before they become lost appointments?

This metric measures the effectiveness of the scheduling and confirmation language your team uses — and it reveals, more clearly than almost any other number, whether patients feel genuinely committed to their appointments or whether the language your team uses is inadvertently giving them permission to cancel.

The confirmation call that asks *"are you still coming?"* creates measurably higher cancellation rates than the confirmation call that says *"we're looking forward to seeing you tomorrow."* If your cancellation rate is higher than ten percent something in your scheduling and confirmation language is leaving a door open that should be gently closed.

Four — Reactivation Success Rate

Of the overdue patients your practice contacts in any given month what percentage schedule an appointment as a result of that contact?

This metric measures both the quality of the reactivation language and the health of the patient relationship — because patients who feel genuinely connected to their practice respond to outreach differently than patients who feel like a name on a list.

A reactivation success rate below twenty percent almost always indicates language that is triggering guilt or defensiveness rather than connection. A rate above thirty-five percent indicates a practice whose communication has built enough trust that even patients who have been away for a while feel welcomed back rather than judged.

Five — Patient Retention Rate

What percentage of your active patients return for their next scheduled appointment within the recommended timeframe?

This is the long-game metric — the one that tells you whether the patient relationship your team is building with its language is strong enough to keep people coming back year after year. High retention rates are the ultimate validation of a communication culture that makes patients feel valued. Low retention rates — particularly when not driven by obvious external factors like relocation or demographics — are almost always a communication story in disguise.

Setting Goals That Create Accountability Without Creating Fear

There is a right way and a wrong way to introduce communication metrics and goals into a dental practice — and the difference between them determines whether the team embraces the process or resists it.

The wrong way is to present the metrics as evidence of failure. To hold up a 54 percent new patient conversion rate as proof that the front desk team is underperforming. To share a 61 percent case acceptance rate as an indictment of the clinical team's communication skills.

This approach — however well-intentioned — activates the same defensive response in team members that shame-based language activates in patients. It closes people down rather than opening them up. And closed people do not improve. They protect.

The right way is to present metrics as information — neutral, non-judgmental data that tells the practice where it currently stands and gives it a specific, exciting target to move toward.

"Here is where we are. Here is where we want to be. Here is what we are going to do together to get there."

That framing turns a performance gap into a growth opportunity. And growth opportunities — particularly when the path to growth is clear and the tools to achieve it are readily available — motivate teams in ways that performance pressure never can.

John Maxwell writes with characteristic clarity on this distinction:

"People don't care how much you know until they know how much you care."

The leader who introduces communication goals from a foundation of genuine care for the team's development — who says in effect *"I want to give you the tools to do this better and then celebrate with you when you do"* — will get a fundamentally different response than the leader who introduces goals as accountability mechanisms designed to surface underperformance.

Same goals. Entirely different culture around them.

The Monthly Communication Review

One of the most powerful and most underutilized practices in dental office management is the monthly communication review — a dedicated, structured conversation between leadership and team that uses the five communication metrics as its foundation.

Not a production meeting. Not a numbers review. A communication review — specifically focused on how the practice is talking to its patients, what is working, what needs attention, and what the team is going to focus on improving in the coming month.

In an A.L.I.G.N.™ practice this meeting has a consistent structure.

It opens with celebration. What improved since last month? Where did the team see the language training working? Who had a conversation that went particularly well — and what did they say that made it work? Celebrating wins first is not soft management. It is neurologically intelligent leadership. People who feel recognized for improvement are neurologically primed to keep improving.

It continues with honest assessment. Where are the metrics still below target? Not as an accusation but as a question — what is happening in this area, and what do we think is driving it? This is the space for the kind of honest team conversation that only happens in a culture where measurement is used for growth rather than punishment.

It closes with focus. Of all the areas where improvement is possible what is the one thing the team is going to focus on most intentionally in the coming month? Not five things. Not a comprehensive overhaul. One thing — specific, achievable, and directly connected to a measurable outcome.

That one thing — practiced consistently for thirty days — produces more sustainable improvement than any amount of comprehensive training applied inconsistently.

As John Maxwell writes:

"Motivation gets you going but discipline keeps you growing."

The monthly communication review is the container for that consistency. It keeps the team's attention on the right things. It keeps the improvement happening. And it keeps the culture of intentional communication alive and growing rather than fading between annual training events.

Goals and the Morning Huddle

The morning huddle — discussed briefly in the Awareness chapter — becomes a significantly more powerful tool when it is connected to the practice's communication goals.

A goal-aware morning huddle does not just review the day's schedule. It identifies the communication opportunities and challenges the day presents — and prepares the team specifically for them.

"We have three new patients today. Let's make sure every one of them hears a warm, specific welcome when they arrive — not just 'sign in here.'"

"We have two patients on the schedule with unscheduled treatment from their last visit. Let's make sure we create a natural opportunity to revisit that conversation today."

"We've been working on our confirmation language this month. Before you make today's calls let's take two minutes to practice the new approach together."

These are not lengthy additions to the huddle. They take minutes. And they keep the communication goals present in the team's awareness on the days when it matters most — the days when the schedule is full and the phones are ringing and the easiest thing in the world would be to default to old habits.

Goals that live only in monthly review meetings fade between meetings. Goals that are touched daily — however briefly — stay alive in the team's awareness and shape their behavior in real time.

That is the difference between a goal that decorates a meeting agenda and a goal that actually drives change.

Connecting Communication Goals to Financial Outcomes

One of the most motivating things a practice can do — for both leadership and team — is make the financial impact of communication improvements visible.

Not as pressure. As possibility.

When a team can see that improving their new patient phone conversion rate from 58 percent to 72 percent — on just eight new patient calls per week — means four additional new patients per month, and that those four patients represent a conservative $8,000 in immediate production and potentially $80,000 in lifetime value, the goal stops being abstract.

It becomes personal.

Because those are not just numbers. They are the patients who get the care they need. They are the production that funds the team's compensation review. They are the referrals that reduce the marketing budget. They are the reviews that make the next new patient's decision easier.

Communication goals connected to financial outcomes create a team that understands — viscerally and specifically — why the words matter. Not because they were told the words matter. Because they can see exactly what the right words are worth.

John Maxwell writes:

"Leaders become great not because of their power but because of their ability to empower others."

Giving your team visibility into the financial impact of their communication is an act of empowerment. It says — explicitly and powerfully — that what they do every day matters. That the phone call they handle at 8:47 on a Tuesday morning is not a small administrative task. It is a moment with real consequence. Real value. Real impact.

Teams that understand that show up differently.

They handle the difficult call with more care. They practice the new language with more motivation. They celebrate the improved metric with genuine pride — because they know what it cost to earn it and what it means for the practice they have built together.

That is what goals do when they are set right, tracked honestly, and connected to something that genuinely matters.

They do not just measure performance.

They create meaning.

A Note on Patience

Before we close this chapter, I want to say something that does not get said often enough in practice management conversations:

Communication improvement takes time.

Not forever. Not years. But more time than a single training session, a single month of focus, or a single excellent morning huddle.

Language habits — particularly deeply ingrained ones — do not change overnight. The scheduling coordinator who has been saying *"are you still coming?"* for six years will not fully replace that habit in two weeks. The hygienist who defaults to blame language around home care will not permanently shift to coaching language after one team meeting.

Real habit change — the kind that becomes automatic, that survives a busy day and a difficult patient and a staffing shortage — takes consistent practice over a sustained period. Research on habit formation suggests that meaningful behavioral change typically requires between sixty and ninety days of consistent practice before the new behavior becomes genuinely automatic.

This means that goal timelines in A.L.I.G.N.™ language training should be set with that reality in mind. Not thirty days to transform the practice. Ninety days to meaningfully move one metric. Six months to see the full impact of a focused language initiative. A year to look back and recognize that the practice communicates in a fundamentally different — and measurably better — way than it did twelve months ago.

John Maxwell speaks to this with the kind of long-game wisdom that permeates his best work:

"The secret of your success is determined by your daily agenda."

The daily agenda of a practice committed to communication goals is simple. Practice the language in the morning huddle. Track the metrics weekly. Review the progress monthly. Celebrate every genuine improvement. Adjust what is not working. Repeat.

Day after day. Week after week. Month after month.

Until one day — without dramatic announcement or ceremonial milestone — the practice looks up and realizes that the conversations happening today are simply different from the ones that were happening a year ago.

Better. Warmer. More consistent. More effective.

And the patients are noticing.

That day — quiet and unremarkable and profoundly significant — is the day the goals did their work.

Chapter Takeaway

Goals in the A.L.I.G.N.™ framework are not just financial targets — they are communication targets, specifically designed to measure the quality of the conversations that drive every financial outcome in the practice. The five communication metrics that matter most — new patient phone conversion, case acceptance, cancellation and no-show rate, reactivation success, and patient retention — provide a real-time picture of practice communication health and create specific, exciting targets for improvement. Goals set with care, tracked consistently, and connected to meaningful outcomes do not just measure performance. They create a team that understands the value of their work, takes pride in their improvement, and shows up every day with the kind of intentionality that transforms a practice from the inside out. Vague goals produce vague results. Specific goals, honestly tracked and genuinely celebrated, produce something else entirely — a practice that grows with purpose, direction, and the full engagement of every person on the team.

What This Means for Your Practice

The moment that never gets old — no matter how many times I have watched it happen — is the moment a practice owner pulls the metrics six weeks into an A.L.I.G.N.™ implementation and sees the numbers move.

Not abstractly. Specifically. The new patient conversion rate that has been sitting at fifty-four percent for three years sitting at sixty-eight percent. The case acceptance rate that plateaued at sixty-two percent climbing to seventy-four. The cancellation rate dropping four points in a single month.

And they look at me and say — that is from the phone language? Yes. That is from the phone language.

That moment — when the invisible daily work of language training becomes visible in the numbers — is the most powerful confirmation available that the work is real.

-Here's What I Want You to Remember-

Pull your new patient conversion rate right now. Write it down. Date it.

That number is your starting line. And I promise you — if you implement what this book describes with genuine consistency — it is going to look different in ninety days.

Hold onto it. Because the distance between where it is today and where it is ninety days from now is the story of what your team's communication development actually produced.

And that story is worth knowing specifically.

Chapter 9

N is for Navigation

Building Systems That Outlast Any One Person

"A leader who produces other leaders multiplies their influences." — John Maxwell

There is a particular kind of anxiety that lives in the heart of every practice owner who has successfully implemented a positive change in their practice.

It is quieter than the anxiety that came before the change. Less urgent. Less visible. But in many ways more insidious — because it arrives at precisely the moment when everything seems to be working, when the team is communicating well and the metrics are moving in the right direction and the morning huddle actually feels like the energizing ritual it was always supposed to be.

The anxiety sounds like this:

"What happens when Sarah leaves?"

Or — *"What happens when I bring in a new team member who has not been through any of this training?"*

Or — *"What happens when we get busy and the pressure builds and everyone defaults back to their old habits because the new ones have not been practiced enough to be truly automatic?"*

Or simply — *"How do I make sure this sticks?"*

That anxiety is not paranoia. It is wisdom. Because the history of practice improvement in dentistry is littered with genuinely good initiatives that produced genuine results for three to six months and then quietly dissolved — not because they were wrong, but because they were never built into the infrastructure of the practice in a way that could survive the inevitable pressures of time, turnover, and the relentless demands of running a busy clinical operation.

Training that is not systematized is temporary by definition.

Culture that depends on any one person's presence — including the practice owner's — is one resignation letter away from collapse.

The Navigation pillar of A.L.I.G.N.™ exists to solve this problem. Permanently.

"The pessimist complains about the wind. The optimist expects it to change. The leader adjusts the sails." — John Maxwell

What Navigation Actually Means

Navigation in the A.L.I.G.N.™ framework is the process of embedding everything the practice has learned — the awareness, the language, the identity, the goals — into systems, structures, and processes that operate independently of any individual person's memory, motivation, or continued presence.

It is the difference between a practice that communicates well because Sarah is there and a practice that communicates well because the system requires it, supports it, measures it, and reinforces it regardless of who is in the building on any given day.

It is the difference between a culture that was installed by a consultant and a culture that has become the practice's own — so deeply woven into how things are done here that a new team member absorbs it within their first week not because anyone gave them a manual but because everything around them models it consistently and without exception.

It is, ultimately, the difference between a practice that improves and a practice that transforms.

Improvement is temporary. Transformation is structural.

Navigation is what makes transformation structural.

John Maxwell writes:

"Systems run the world. Leaders run the systems. And systems create results."

The Navigation pillar is about building the right systems — communication systems, onboarding systems, accountability systems, review systems — so that A.L.I.G.N.™ is not something the practice does occasionally. It is something the practice is, continuously, regardless of which team members are there to carry it.

The Four Navigation Systems

In an A.L.I.G.N.™ practice Navigation is built through four interconnected systems — each one addressing a different aspect of how the culture is maintained, grown, and transmitted over time.

System One — The Onboarding System

Every new team member who joins a practice is either an opportunity or a risk.

They are an opportunity if the practice has a clear, intentional onboarding system that immerses them in the communication culture from day one — giving them the language, the principles, the standard, and the context to communicate consistently with patients and colleagues from their very first interaction.

They are a risk if the practice's onboarding process amounts to shadowing an existing team member for a few days and hoping they absorb the good habits along with the inevitable bad ones.

Most dental practices — even good ones — fall into the second category. Onboarding is an afterthought. New team members are hired for their clinical skill or their customer service experience and then thrown into the daily flow of the practice with minimal guidance about how this practice specifically communicates with its patients.

The result is entirely predictable. New team members default to whatever communication habits they brought with them from their previous positions — some of which align with the practice's culture and some of which quietly work against it — while the practice owner wonders why the communication improvements they worked so hard to implement seem to dilute a little with every new hire.

An A.L.I.G.N.™ onboarding system addresses this directly. It is not a lengthy or complicated process. It requires three components.

A communication culture document. Not a mission statement. A living document that describes specifically how this practice communicates — the language it uses, the tone it maintains, the standard it holds itself to, and the why behind all of it. Clear enough for a new team member to understand. Specific enough to guide their actual behavior. Meaningful enough that reading it tells them something true and important about the place they have just joined.

A structured observation period. New team members learn more from watching than from being told. But the watching must be structured — not random observation of whoever happens to be available, but deliberate exposure to the practice's best communicators in its highest-stakes moments. The new scheduling coordinator should hear five new patient phone calls handled expertly before she handles her first one alone. The new dental assistant should observe three treatment presentations before she participates in one. Structured observation is the fastest and most effective way to transmit communication culture to a new team member.

An early feedback loop. New team members need to know quickly — not at the ninety-day review — whether their communication is aligned with the practice's standard. Not a punitive assessment. A supportive check-in. How are you feeling in these conversations? Is there anything you are finding difficult? Let me listen to a few calls with you and share what I notice.

Early feedback prevents small misalignments from becoming entrenched habits. And it signals to the new team member — in the most powerful way possible — that communication is taken seriously in this practice. That it is not an afterthought. That it is as important as any clinical or administrative skill they were hired for.

System Two — The Huddle System

The morning huddle has appeared throughout this book because it is the single most powerful daily communication touchpoint available to any dental practice — and the most consistently underutilized.

In the Navigation framework the morning huddle is not just a scheduling review. It is the primary daily vehicle for keeping the communication culture alive and growing — the moment each day when the team reconnects with the standard, prepares for the specific communication opportunities the day holds, and reinforces the language habits they are building together.

An A.L.I.G.N.™ huddle system has a consistent structure that takes no more than ten to fifteen minutes and accomplishes five things.

Schedule review with a communication lens. Not just who is coming in and what procedures are scheduled — but what does each patient on today's schedule need from us communicatively? The anxious patient. The patient with unscheduled treatment. The new patient coming in for the first time. The patient who called yesterday with a financial concern. Each of these patients needs something specific from the team today — and the huddle is where that preparation happens.

Language focus. One phrase. One principle. One specific communication scenario to practice. Not a comprehensive language training session — a two-minute focus on the one thing the team is working on this week. *"This week we're practicing our confirmation call language. Let's take sixty seconds and say it out loud together before we start."* Repetition is how habits form. The huddle is where that repetition happens daily.

Win sharing. One positive communication moment from the previous day. A patient who responded well to the new treatment presentation language. A confirmation call that felt natural for the first time. A reactivation call that resulted in a scheduled appointment. Thirty seconds of celebration keeps the team connected to the impact of their language work and motivated to keep improving.

Challenge surfacing. Is there anything coming up today that feels communicatively difficult? A patient the team expects to be unhappy. A financial conversation that needs careful handling. A treatment recommendation that has been declined before and needs a fresh approach. The huddle is where these challenges are identified and the team prepares together — so nobody faces a difficult communication moment alone and unprepared.

Intention setting. How do we want our patients to feel when they leave today? Not what do we want to produce or how many cases do we want to close. How do we want people to feel? That question — asked every morning and answered together — keeps the team's focus exactly where it needs to be. On the patient. On the relationship. On the thing that drives everything else.

Ten minutes. Every morning. Without exception.

That consistency — the dailiness of it — is what makes the huddle a navigation system rather than a periodic training event. It keeps the culture present in the team's awareness on the days when it would be easiest to let it slide.

And there will be days when it would be easiest to let it slide. The schedule is chaotic. A team member called in sick. The lab case is not back. On those days the huddle feels like one more thing to do in a morning that already has too many things.

Those are exactly the days when the huddle matters most.

Because those are the days when teams under pressure default to their lowest communication habits — and the huddle is what keeps the standard present even when the pressure is highest.

John Maxwell writes:

"Successful and unsuccessful people do not vary greatly in their abilities. They vary in their desires to reach their potential."

The daily huddle is the daily expression of the practice's desire to reach its potential. It is ten minutes that say — every single morning, regardless of what else is happening — *"this matters to us. The way we talk to people matters. And we are going to take a moment to be intentional about it before the day begins."*

That intention — sustained daily over months and years — is what turns a trained team into a transformed practice.

System Three — The Performance Conversation System

In most dental practices performance conversations happen in two scenarios:

When something goes badly wrong. And at the annual review.

Neither of these is a system. Both of them are reactive responses to the absence of a system. And both of them — however well-intentioned — produce the kind of defensive, high-stakes conversations that are least likely to result in genuine growth.

The performance conversation that happens in response to a crisis is inherently charged with urgency and emotion — the worst possible conditions for coaching. The annual review that attempts to address twelve months of accumulated performance in a single sixty-minute conversation is structurally incapable of producing the kind of specific, timely feedback that actually changes behavior.

An A.L.I.G.N.™ performance conversation system replaces both of these with something simpler, more frequent, and infinitely more effective:

Regular, brief, specific, growth-oriented conversations — connected directly to the communication metrics and goals the practice is tracking.

Not annual reviews. Monthly check-ins. Not crisis responses. Proactive coaching conversations. Not evaluations. Collaborative growth discussions.

The structure is straightforward.

What is working? Specifically and genuinely. Not a warm-up platitude before the real conversation. A genuine acknowledgment of what the team member is doing well — with enough specificity that they know you have actually been paying attention.

What is one thing to focus on? Not a comprehensive list of improvements. One thing. The most important thing. The thing that — if improved over the next thirty days — will have the most meaningful impact on this team member's communication effectiveness and the patients' experience.

What support do they need? What can leadership provide — in language guidance, in observation opportunities, in practice time, in encouragement — to help this team member improve in that one area? The conversation is not complete until this question is answered. Because a team member who knows what to improve but does not know how to improve it has been given a destination without a map.

How will we know it is improving? Back to the metrics. Back to the measurable. What specific evidence will tell both the leader and the team member that progress is happening? This question keeps the coaching conversation connected to reality rather than floating in the comfortable abstraction of good intentions.

These conversations take twenty minutes. They happen monthly. They replace the anxiety-producing annual review with a rhythm of ongoing growth that team members — particularly good ones — find motivating rather than threatening.

John Maxwell is direct about what this kind of leadership produces:

"The greatest day in your life and mine is when we take total responsibility for our attitudes. That's the day we truly grow up."

A performance conversation system built on growth rather than judgment creates team members who take responsibility for their communication development — not because they are afraid of consequences but because they are genuinely invested in their own improvement and in the practice they are helping to build.

That investment — freely given, genuinely felt — is worth more than any performance management system ever designed.

System Four — The Evolution System

The fourth navigation system addresses something that most practice management frameworks completely ignore:

The practice will change. The team will change. The patient population will change. The market will change. And the communication challenges the practice faces in five years will not be identical to the ones it faces today.

A navigation system that is built only for the practice as it currently exists is a system that will eventually become obsolete — not because it was wrong, but because it was static in a dynamic environment.

The A.L.I.G.N.™ Evolution System is the practice's mechanism for staying current — for regularly examining whether the communication framework is keeping pace with the practice's growth and the world's changes and updating it when it is not.

It has three components.

The quarterly communication audit. Every three months the practice conducts a deliberate review of its communication systems — not just the metrics, but the language itself. Are there new situations arising in patient conversations that the current framework does not address? Are there phrases in the team's repertoire that are working less effectively than they once did? Are there shifts in patient demographics, insurance landscapes, or practice offerings that require new communication approaches?

The quarterly audit keeps the framework alive rather than fossilizing it. It treats communication as a living system that requires ongoing cultivation rather than a fixed solution that was installed once and never needs revisiting.

The annual culture assessment. Once a year the practice steps back from the day-to-day and asks a larger question: Who are we now — as a practice, as a team, as a communication culture — compared to who we were a year ago? What has improved? What has regressed? What has changed about our patient population, our team composition, or our practice identity that needs to be reflected in how we communicate?

The annual culture assessment is not a performance review. It is a strategic conversation about the practice's identity and direction — the kind of conversation that most practices never have because they are too busy managing the present to examine where they are going.

The new challenge protocol. When something new arises — a significant shift in insurance reimbursement, a new service offering, a change in the competitive landscape, a patient demographic shift — the practice has a clear process for developing the communication response to that change rather than waiting for team members to figure it out individually.

The new challenge protocol says: when something changes that affects how we talk to patients we address it as a team, deliberately and proactively, before it becomes an inconsistency in the patient experience.

Together these three components ensure that the A.L.I.G.N.™ framework is not a snapshot of how the practice communicated at a single moment in time. It is a living system that grows and adapts with the practice — getting stronger with age rather than more outdated.

When Systems Become Culture

There is a moment — and every practice that builds genuine navigation systems eventually reaches it — when the systems stop feeling like systems.

They stop feeling like processes to follow and structures to maintain and checklists to complete. They simply feel like how things are done here.

The morning huddle is no longer something the team does because the practice owner scheduled it. It is something the team misses on the rare occasions it does not happen — because it has become the rhythm of the day, the container for their shared intention, the moment of connection that makes the work feel meaningful rather than mechanical.

The monthly communication review is no longer a meeting to prepare for. It is the conversation the team looks forward to — because it is one of the few moments in the busy life of a dental practice when everyone stops to look honestly at how they are doing, celebrate what is working, and invest in what is not.

The onboarding process is no longer something the office manager coordinates when a new hire starts. It is the culture welcoming a new member — passing on not just information but identity, not just skills but values, not just procedures but the genuine pride of a team that knows who it is and how it communicates.

When systems become culture something remarkable happens to the practice's relationship with change.

Change — which is the enemy of most practice cultures because most practice cultures depend on stability to maintain their current performance — becomes an opportunity. New team member? The culture will shape them. New services? The culture will communicate them. New challenges? The culture will navigate them.

Because the culture is no longer fragile. It is structural. It is built into the bones of the practice — into its daily rhythms and its monthly reviews and its onboarding processes and its performance conversations — in a way that can absorb change and growth and difficulty without losing its essential character.

John Maxwell captures this with words that land differently once you have built something real enough to need protecting:

"Change is inevitable. Growth is optional."

Navigation makes growth not just possible but inevitable — because it builds the infrastructure that turns the inevitable changes every practice faces into opportunities for the culture to prove its strength rather than threats to its survival.

The Practice That Does Not Depend on You

I want to close this chapter — and the five-pillar section of this book — with a thought that I believe is one of the most important ideas any dental practice owner can genuinely internalize.

The goal of building a great practice is not to build a practice that needs you.

It is to build a practice that reflects you — your values, your standard, your commitment to exceptional care and genuine human connection — while being fully capable of functioning at that level whether you are in the building or not.

That is the Navigation goal. Not a practice that runs itself — clinical excellence will always require skilled, present, engaged clinicians. But a practice whose communication culture, whose patient experience, whose team standard, and whose growth systems are so well built that they do not depend on any one person's memory or motivation or presence to maintain their excellence.

When you have built that practice you have built something that can be expanded. Something that can be led by an empowered team rather than managed by an exhausted owner. Something whose growth is not limited by your personal capacity to be everywhere and do everything.

You have built a practice that is genuinely ready for whatever comes next — growth, transition, expansion, legacy.

You have built something that lasts.

John Maxwell — who has spent his entire career studying what makes leadership and organizations endure — puts it this way:

"The ultimate leader is one who is willing to develop people to the point that they eventually surpass him or her in knowledge and ability."

That is the Navigation vision for A.L.I.G.N.™

Not a practice that depends on the leader's presence to communicate at its best.

A practice whose team has been so well developed — in awareness, in language, in identity, in goals, and in the systems that sustain all of it — that they carry the standard forward with or without the leader's hand on the wheel.

That practice does not just serve its patients better.

It serves them better every year — growing more consistent, more connected, and more capable with every new team member it welcomes, every challenge it navigates, and every patient whose life it touches with the kind of genuine, intentional, trust-building communication that A.L.I.G.N.™ was built to create.

Chapter Takeaway

Navigation is the pillar that makes everything else permanent. It transforms the Awareness, Language, Identity, and Goals work from temporary improvements into structural cultural change — by embedding A.L.I.G.N.™ into four interconnected systems: the Onboarding System that transmits the culture to every new team member from day one, the Huddle System that keeps the language and standard present in daily practice, the Performance Conversation System that supports ongoing individual growth in a coaching rather than evaluative framework, and the Evolution System that keeps the culture alive and current as the practice grows and changes. When these four systems are working together the practice no longer depends on any one person's presence to maintain its communication excellence. It has become something more durable than a trained team. It has become a transformed practice — one whose culture is structural, whose growth is sustainable, and whose impact on every patient it serves compounds with every passing year.

What This Means for Your Practice

Every coaching engagement I have ever delivered has ended.

Not because the work was finished. Because coaching engagements have timelines and budgets and defined completion points. And the moment I walk out of a practice for the last time as the active coach is the moment the practice has to decide what it is actually made of.

The practices that sustain the improvement — that keep improving after I am gone, sometimes for years, sometimes indefinitely — are not the ones with the most talented teams or the most committed dentists or the most favorable market conditions.

They are the ones with the systems. The morning huddle that runs whether I am watching or not. The monthly review that happens whether anyone is pushing for it or not. The onboarding process that transmits the communication culture to the next new hire and the one after that.

-Here's What I Want You to Remember-

Those systems are not supplementary features of A.L.I.G.N.™. They are the mechanism by which everything this methodology builds outlasts the methodology's active delivery.

The Navigation pillar is not the last pillar because it is the least important. It is last because it is the one that makes all the others permanent.

Build the systems. Protect the systems. And the communication culture you build will still be running — stronger than it is today — long after you have forgotten the specific session where it all began.

Chapter 10

The New Patient Experience

You Never Get a Second Chance at a First Impression — But Most Practices Waste the First One

"You never get a second chance to make a first impression — so make the first impression count." — John Maxwell

Somewhere in your city right now a person is sitting at their kitchen table — or standing in a parking lot between errands, or scrolling on their phone during a lunch break — working up the courage to call a dental office.

They have been putting it off. Maybe for months. Maybe longer. The reasons are as varied as people are — dental anxiety that goes back to a childhood experience they still wince at, a gap in insurance coverage that made scheduling feel financially irresponsible, a busy life that kept pushing the appointment to next week and then the week after that, a vague embarrassment about how long it has been since their last visit and what a dentist might say when they see it.

Whatever the reason for the delay the decision to finally make the call represents a genuine act of courage. Small by some measures. Significant by any honest one.

And in approximately forty-five seconds that courage will either be rewarded or confirmed as misplaced — entirely depending on the words spoken by the person who picks up the phone.

This is the new patient experience. And it begins not in the reception area, not at the front desk, not in the operatory — but in that forty-five second window when a stranger decides whether your practice is a place they want to trust with their health.

Most practices have never thought about it in those terms.

The ones that have are the ones with the waitlists.

"Connecting is the ability to identify with people and relate to them in a way that increases your influence with them." — John Maxwell

What New Patients Are Actually Asking

When a new patient calls a dental practice and asks *"how much is a cleaning and exam?"* they are not actually asking about price.

I want to say that again because it is one of the most important and most consistently misunderstood truths in dental practice communication:

When a new patient asks about price they are not primarily asking about price.

They are asking — in the only language they have available to them in that moment — a much deeper and more personal question:

"Is there a place for me here?"

The price question is the vehicle. The real question is about belonging. About safety. About whether the person on the other end of this call is going to make them feel welcome or make them feel like a transaction.

A person who feels welcomed and valued will schedule an appointment even if the fees are slightly higher than they expected. A person who feels dismissed or inconvenienced will not schedule even if the fees are the lowest in the market.

This is not a theory. It is the observed reality of thousands of new patient phone interactions — and it explains why practices that handle the new patient call with warmth and genuine engagement consistently out-convert practices that handle it efficiently but impersonally, regardless of their relative fee structures.

The new patient is not shopping for the cheapest dentist. They are shopping for the one they can trust.

And trust is communicated — or destroyed — in the first forty-five seconds of the first phone call.

Dale Carnegie understood this principle long before the dental practice management industry existed:

"You can make more friends in two months by becoming interested in other people than you can in two years by trying to get other people interested in you."

The new patient phone call is the moment to be interested in them. Not to be efficient. Not to be informative. Not to be accurate about fees or availability or insurance participation.

To be interested. Genuinely, warmly, specifically interested in this person and what they need.

Everything else follows from that.

The Anatomy of a Perfect New Patient Call

What does a genuinely excellent new patient phone call actually look and sound like in practice?

It has five elements — each one building on the one before it to create an experience of welcome that makes scheduling feel like the obvious and comfortable next step.

Element One — The Warm Opening.

The call begins before the patient speaks. The tone of the greeting — the energy, the warmth, the genuine sense that this call is welcome rather than an interruption — sets the emotional temperature for everything that follows.

"Thank you for calling [Practice Name], this is [Name] — how can I help you today?"

Simple. Warm. Personal. The team member's name matters more than most people realize — it immediately humanizes the interaction and signals that the patient is speaking with a person rather than a system.

What it is not: *"[Practice Name], please hold."* Or a rushed, flat delivery that communicates — regardless of the words — that this call arrived at a bad time.

The warm opening is not about performance. It is about presence. The team member who answers the phone needs to be genuinely present for that call — not managing three other tasks simultaneously, not mentally still in the previous conversation, not checking the schedule while half-listening.

Present. Warm. Ready.

Element Two — The Discovery.

Before answering any question the excellent communicator asks one.

Not a scripted intake question. A genuine expression of interest in who this person is and what they need.

"I'd be happy to help with that. Can I ask — are you looking to establish care with us as a new patient?"

Or — *"Of course. Is this your first time reaching out to our practice?"*

This question does two things simultaneously. It gathers information that will shape the conversation. And it communicates to the caller that they are being seen as a person — not processed as an inquiry.

Most new patient callers are slightly surprised by a genuine discovery question. They called expecting to ask their question and receive an answer. Being asked something first — something that expresses interest in them — creates a small but meaningful moment of connection that changes the entire texture of the conversation.

Element Three — The Acknowledgment.

Whatever the patient's situation — first dental visit in two years, long-term dental anxiety, recent move to the area, specific concern about a tooth — it deserves acknowledgment before it receives a response.

"It's great that you're reaching out — it sounds like getting established with a good dental home is something that's been on your mind."

Or — *"I completely understand. A lot of our patients felt the same way before their first visit with us."*

Acknowledgment is not agreement. It is not validation of a choice or a situation. It is simply the communication that the patient's experience — whatever it is — has been heard and received without judgment.

That experience of being heard without judgment — particularly for patients who carry shame or anxiety about their dental history — is often the single most powerful moment in the entire new patient phone call. It is the moment the wall comes down.

Element Four — The Confidence.

After acknowledgment comes confidence — the clear, warm, genuine communication that this practice is capable of helping this patient and is genuinely glad they called.

"We'd love to have you come in. Let me tell you a little about what your first visit would look like so you know exactly what to expect."

Or — *"We work with patients in all kinds of situations and we're very good at making sure you're comfortable every step of the way."*

Confidence is not arrogance. It is not an aggressive sales pitch. It is the quiet assurance of a practice that knows what it does well and communicates that knowledge in a way that makes the patient feel safe rather than sold to.

The confident response to a new patient call says — without saying it explicitly — *"you called the right place."* And patients who feel they called the right place schedule appointments. Patients who are still uncertain whether they called the right place ask more questions, hesitate, and frequently call the next number on their list.

Element Five — The Invitation.

The call closes with a clear, warm, assumptive invitation to schedule — not a question about whether the patient wants to schedule, but a natural movement toward finding the right time.

"Let's find a time that works perfectly for you. Do mornings or afternoons tend to work better?"

Not — *"Would you like to schedule an appointment?"* That question invites a yes or a no. The assumptive invitation assumes the yes — which is the appropriate assumption when the previous four elements have been executed well — and moves directly to the practical question of when.

The assumptive invitation does not pressure the patient. It simply reflects the natural next step in a conversation that has gone well — and most patients, having experienced the warmth and competence of the previous four elements, are entirely ready to take that step.

Five elements. One phone call. The beginning of a patient relationship that — if everything that follows lives up to the promise of this conversation — could last decades.

The Courage to Address the Elephant in the Room

One of the most common and most costly mistakes in new patient communication is the avoidance of the obvious.

The patient who calls and mentions they have not been to the dentist in three years. The patient who leads with *"I know I've been putting this off."* The patient who says — directly or indirectly — that they are anxious, embarrassed, or hesitant.

Many dental teams, sensing the emotional sensitivity of these moments, respond with cheerful deflection. *"Oh don't worry, we'll take great care of you!"* Said brightly. Said kindly. Said in a way that completely fails to acknowledge what the patient actually just shared.

The patient who says *"I'm a little embarrassed about how long it's been"* is not looking for cheerful reassurance. They are testing the water — seeing whether this practice is safe enough to be honest with. And a response that skips past their honesty without acknowledging it fails that test quietly but completely.

The response that passes the test sounds like this:

"Please don't be — you'd be surprised how many of our patients have felt the same way. The important thing is that you're reaching out now, and we're genuinely glad you did."

That response does three things in two sentences. It normalizes the patient's experience without minimizing it. It redirects from the past to the present — from the gap in care to the decision to address it. And it communicates genuine welcome — not the performative welcome of a business greeting but the real welcome of a place that actually wants this person there.

Patients who feel genuinely welcomed despite their circumstances — despite their anxiety, their embarrassment, their gap in care, their complicated insurance situation — do not just schedule appointments.

They become the most loyal patients in the practice.

Because loyalty is built not in the easy moments but in the moments when a practice had the grace to make someone feel valued when they expected to feel judged.

Brené Brown writes:

"Connection is the energy that exists between people when they feel seen, heard, and valued — when they can give and receive without judgment."

The new patient phone call — at its best — is an act of connection in exactly Brown's sense. The patient is seen. Heard. Valued. Received without judgment. And in that moment of genuine connection the patient relationship begins — not at the first appointment, not at the first cleaning, not at the treatment presentation.

Here. On the phone. In the first forty-five seconds.

When They Walk Through the Door

The phone call creates the expectation. The arrival experience must fulfill it.

A patient who had a warm, welcoming, personalized phone call experience arrives at the practice carrying that experience with them — and their nervous system is paying attention to whether what they find matches what they were promised.

If they walk in and are greeted with *"sign in"* — directed to a clipboard without eye contact, without acknowledgment, without the human warmth that the phone call suggested they would find — something deflates. Not dramatically. Not in a way they would necessarily articulate. But the gap between the promise and the reality registers. And registered gaps erode trust.

The arrival greeting for a new patient is not a logistical moment. It is a fulfillment moment — the first opportunity to deliver on the promise of the phone call.

"Good morning — are you [Name]? We've been looking forward to meeting you. Welcome."

Three sentences. Thirty seconds. The patient's name — which communicates that they were expected, that they matter, that someone took the time to know who was coming in today. The phrase *"we've been looking forward to meeting you"* — which communicates that their presence is valued, not merely tolerated. And *"welcome"* — which is not a word most dental practices use and which lands with quiet but genuine power every time it is spoken sincerely.

John Maxwell writes:

"People don't care how much you know until they know how much you care."

The arrival greeting is the first in-person demonstration that the practice cares. And it costs nothing — no technology, no training budget, no operational change. Only the decision to be present, to be warm, and to treat the arrival of a new patient as the genuinely significant moment it is.

The Nervous Patient

No new patient communication scenario is more important — or more consistently mishandled — than the patient who arrives carrying genuine dental anxiety.

Dental anxiety is extraordinarily common. Research suggests that somewhere between thirty and forty percent of adults experience meaningful anxiety about dental care — with a smaller but significant percentage experiencing anxiety severe enough to cause them to avoid dental care entirely until pain or emergency forces them back.

These patients are not difficult. They are vulnerable. And the way a practice responds to that vulnerability in the first moments of the first visit determines not just whether they will return — but whether they will ever be able to receive the care their oral health requires.

The most common response to a patient who expresses dental anxiety is well-intentioned and deeply unhelpful:

"Oh, there's nothing to worry about."

This response — said with genuine kindness by team members who are trying to reduce the patient's distress — actually increases it. Here is why.

When a person shares a fear and is told there is nothing to fear they do not feel reassured. They feel dismissed. The implicit message of *"there's nothing to worry about"* is *"your fear is not valid."* And a person whose fear has been invalidated does not relax. They tense. They feel alone in their anxiety. And they stop sharing — which means the practice has lost its best opportunity to understand what this patient specifically needs in order to feel safe.

The response that actually helps sounds very different:

"I completely understand — and I want you to know that we hear that from a lot of our patients. We're going to take really good care of you today, and the most important thing to us is that you feel comfortable every step of the way. If at any point you need us to slow down or stop just let us know — you are completely in control."

That response does something the dismissive reassurance cannot. It validates the fear. It normalizes it. It communicates that the practice has experience with anxious patients and knows how to care for them. And most powerfully — it gives the patient control. And control is the single most effective antidote to dental anxiety that any practice has available to it.

The patient who feels in control is not the same patient who walked through the door. They are calmer, more trusting, and more open to the care the practice is offering. They are beginning — perhaps for the first time — to experience the dental office as a safe place.

That experience — carefully cultivated in this first visit — is the foundation of a relationship that can change the trajectory of their oral health entirely.

The Late Arrival

Even the new patient who arrives late deserves a first impression worth keeping.

The late arrival is a moment of high vulnerability for a new patient. They are already anxious about being somewhere unfamiliar. Now they are anxious about having inconvenienced a practice they have not yet won the trust of. They arrive at the front desk braced for reproach — because reproach is what their internal critic has been delivering since they realized they were running behind.

"I'm so sorry I'm late" is not an opening statement. It is an apology wrapped in a plea — please do not make this worse than it already feels.

The response that makes it worse: *"You're late."* Or the slightly softer but equally unhelpful: *"We might not be able to see you for the full appointment."*

The response that makes it better — and that sets the patient relationship on the right foundation despite the difficult start:

"We're so glad you made it. Let's see how we can make the most of the time we have — and we'll get you taken care of."

That response does something extraordinary. It eliminates the shame the patient was bracing for. It redirects immediately from the problem to the solution. And it communicates — in seven words — that the practice is focused on this patient's care rather than its own inconvenience.

A new patient who arrives late and is received with grace does not just feel relieved. They feel genuinely surprised — because grace in a moment where criticism would have been understandable is one of the most powerful trust-building experiences available to any relationship.

They will remember it.

They will tell people about it.

And they will come back — reliably, loyally, referringly — to the place that made them feel valued on a day when they felt certain they would feel anything but.

The Paperwork Moment

Every new patient faces it. The clipboard. The forms. The several minutes of administrative processing that stands between their arrival and the beginning of actual care.

For most practices this moment is managed purely logistically. Here are the forms. There is a pen. The waiting room is there.

For an A.L.I.G.N.™ practice this moment is managed humanly.

The patient who arrives and admits — with visible embarrassment — *"I forgot to fill out the forms online"* is not a problem to be managed. They are a person in a moment of mild distress who needs a thirty-second response that removes the shame from the situation entirely.

"No problem at all — we'll help you get everything taken care of right here. It won't take long at all."

Not *"you were supposed to complete that already."* Not even a slightly impatient pause before pivoting to the solution.

Just: no problem. We've got you.

Those four words — and the warmth with which they are spoken — transform a mildly mortifying administrative moment into a small but genuine experience of being cared for. And small experiences of being cared for accumulate. They build the patient's trust deposit with the practice — the emotional reserve that makes them willing to say yes to treatment, willing to return for hygiene, willing to refer the people they love.

Trust is not built in grand gestures. It is built in exactly these moments — the paperwork moment, the late arrival moment, the nervous patient moment, the insurance question moment — when the practice had the option to be efficient or to be human and chose to be human.

Every time.

What the New Patient Experience Is Really About

I want to close this chapter with something that goes deeper than phone scripts and arrival greetings and paperwork protocols.

The new patient experience — at its core — is about one thing.

It is about whether the person who reached out to your practice, despite their anxiety and their uncertainty and whatever barriers stood between them and that call, feels — by the end of their first interaction — that they made the right decision.

Not the right financial decision. Not the right logistical decision. The right human decision.

The decision to trust you.

Every element of the new patient experience — the phone call, the arrival greeting, the response to their anxiety, the handling of their late arrival, the grace around the forgotten paperwork — is either building that sense of rightness or eroding it.

And when the new patient leaves their first visit feeling certain they made the right decision — feeling seen, heard, welcomed, and cared for in a way they did not entirely expect — something happens that no marketing budget in the world can replicate.

They tell someone.

Not because they were asked to. Not because there was a referral incentive or a review request email waiting in their inbox when they got home. But because they had an experience worth talking about — and human beings, by nature, share experiences worth talking about.

Maya Angelou said it and it bears repeating as many times as it takes for it to fully land:

"Try to be a rainbow in someone's cloud."

Make them feel like they called the right place.

Make them feel like they walked into the right practice.

Make them feel like — in a world full of transactional, efficient, impersonal healthcare experiences — they found somewhere that actually sees them as a person.

Do that consistently. With every new patient. On every call. At every arrival. In every moment of vulnerability and paperwork and late arrivals and forgotten forms.

Do that — and the new patient experience becomes your most powerful growth engine.

Not your marketing. Not your technology. Not your fee structure.

The way you make people feel in the first forty-five seconds of the first conversation.

That is everything.

Chapter Takeaway

The new patient experience begins before the patient walks through the door — on the phone call that determines whether they ever do. New patients are not primarily asking about fees or availability or insurance. They are asking whether there is a place for them — whether this practice will make them feel valued, safe, and genuinely welcomed. A.L.I.G.N.™ communication in the new patient experience is built around five elements of the perfect phone call, a fulfillment-focused arrival greeting, and specific, empathy-first responses to the most common new patient scenarios — dental anxiety, late arrivals, and forgotten paperwork. The goal throughout is not efficiency. It is the creation of a feeling — of being seen, heard, and genuinely welcomed — that makes every new patient certain they called the right place. That feeling, created consistently, is the foundation of a patient relationship that lasts decades and generates referrals that no marketing budget can match.

What This Means for Your Practice

The new patient phone call is sixty seconds that most dental practices have never fully examined.

Not because the call is unimportant — every practice owner knows it matters. But because the person handling it was trained by watching the person before them handle it. And somewhere in that chain of inherited observation the specific, intentional, trust-building language that the call deserves got replaced by whatever felt adequate at the time.

Adequate is the enemy of excellent. And on the new patient phone call the difference between adequate and excellent is not just a better patient experience. It is two to three additional patients per week who say yes instead of quietly calling the next practice on their list.

Listen to your new patient calls this week. Not to evaluate. To experience them as the patient experiences them.

-Here's What I Want You to Remember-

Does the person who answers feel genuinely glad the patient called? Does the call end with a scheduled appointment and a patient who feels welcomed — or with a vague invitation to call back if they have more questions?

The answer to that question is worth more than any marketing investment your practice will make this year.

Because the best marketing in the world cannot overcome the sixty seconds that sends the patient somewhere else.

Chapter 11

Scheduling & Appointment Control

The Schedule Is the Heartbeat of the Practice — Protect It with Better Language

"We are what we repeatedly do. Excellence, then, is not an act, but a habit." — John Maxwell

There is a number that every dental practice owner knows intimately — and that almost none of them talk about openly.

It is the number of empty appointment slots that existed in their schedule last month.

Not the ones that were always open. Not the buffer time built in for emergencies or the intentional gaps between complex procedures. The ones that were supposed to be filled. The appointments that were scheduled — confirmed, anticipated, prepared for — and then were not there when the day arrived.

The cancelled appointments. The no-shows. The last-minute reschedules that left a forty-five minute gap at two in the afternoon that the team scrambled to fill and mostly could not.

In the average dental practice that number is larger than anyone is comfortable admitting. Industry research consistently suggests that unplanned schedule gaps — the ones created by cancellations, no-shows, and failed confirmation calls — cost the average practice between $50,000 and $150,000 in lost production annually.

Per year.

From empty chairs.

And here is the part that makes that number both maddening and hopeful in equal measure:

The majority of those empty chairs were created — at least in part — by the language used in scheduling and confirmation conversations.

Not by patients who were fundamentally uncommitted to their care. Not by demographics or insurance changes or the inherent unpredictability of human beings. By specific, identifiable, changeable communication patterns that either reinforce appointment commitment or quietly give patients permission to cancel.

The language created the gap. Different language can close it.

That is what this chapter is about.

"The difference between where we are and where we want to be is created by the changes we are willing to make." — John Maxwell

The Psychology of Appointment Commitment

Before we talk about specific language it is worth understanding something fundamental about how appointment commitment actually works in the human mind.

When a patient schedules a dental appointment they make a decision. In the moment of scheduling that decision feels clear and motivated — the tooth has been bothering them, the hygiene visit is overdue, the treatment has been recommended and the time feels right. They say yes. They take the appointment. They mean it.

Then life happens.

Not dramatically. Not in the form of genuine emergencies — though those occur too. But in the ordinary accumulation of the days between scheduling and appointment — the busy week at work, the child's school event that got added to the calendar, the morning of the appointment when everything feels harder than it did when the appointment was made and the dental office is the thing that has the most flexibility.

In that moment — the moment of wavering commitment — the patient is looking for one of two things:

A reason to keep the appointment. Or a reason to cancel.

And here is the extraordinary truth that most dental practices have never fully grasped:

The language your team used in the scheduling conversation — and the language they use in the confirmation call — determines which of those two things the patient finds.

The scheduling conversation that ends with *"okay, so we have you down for Tuesday at two — and if anything comes up just give us a call"* has just provided a reason to cancel. The phrase *"if anything comes up"* is not an accommodation. It is an exit ramp — a pre-built justification for cancellation that the patient's wavering commitment will use when Tuesday morning arrives and the dental chair feels like the hardest possible place to be.

The scheduling conversation that ends with *"we've reserved this time specifically for you — we'll look forward to seeing you Tuesday at two"* has provided a reason to keep the appointment. The language of reserved time, of specific value, of genuine anticipation — these are subtle but powerful commitment anchors that make the appointment feel worth keeping rather than easy to abandon.

Same Tuesday. Same two o'clock. Same patient.

Completely different commitment level.

John Maxwell writes:

"People change when they hurt enough that they have to, learn enough that they want to, or receive enough that they are able to."

Scheduling language that anchors commitment gives patients enough — enough of a sense of value, enough of a feeling of genuine connection, enough of the practice's authentic investment in their care — that keeping the appointment becomes the natural choice when the moment of wavering arrives.

That is the goal of every scheduling conversation. Not just to put a name in a slot. To create a commitment strong enough to survive the ordinary pressures of life between scheduling and arrival.

The Language of Scheduling

Every scheduling conversation — whether it is a new patient calling for the first time, an existing patient booking their next hygiene visit, or a patient scheduling treatment — has three communication objectives.

First — make the appointment feel valuable.

Not valuable in the abstract sense of "your health is important." Valuable in the specific sense of reserved, anticipated, prepared for. The language of value in scheduling sounds like this:

"We're going to reserve this time specifically for you."

"Dr. [Name] will have this time set aside just for your care."

"We'll make sure everything is ready for you when you arrive."

These phrases do something subtle but significant. They shift the appointment from a slot in a schedule — interchangeable, replaceable, essentially anonymous — to a reserved commitment. A specific allocation of the practice's time and attention that has meaning and weight.

Patients who feel their appointment has been reserved for them specifically experience a measurably higher psychological barrier to cancellation than patients who feel they simply have a time slot. The language of reservation creates a sense of reciprocal obligation — not a burden, but the natural human response to being told that someone has set something aside specifically for you.

Second — make the patient feel anticipated.

"We're looking forward to seeing you."

"We'll see you Tuesday — the team will be glad to have you in."

"We're excited to get started on this for you."

These are not empty pleasantries. They are commitment anchors — small but genuine expressions of anticipation that make the patient feel expected. And people who feel expected show up.

Think about the difference in your own experience between arriving somewhere where you feel expected — where someone is ready for you, glad to see you, genuinely anticipating your presence — versus arriving somewhere where you are simply the next name on a list. The feeling is entirely different. The commitment to not letting someone down who is genuinely looking forward to seeing you is a more powerful motivator than almost any reminder or confirmation system a practice could implement.

Third — close without creating an exit.

The scheduling conversation must close in a way that assumes the appointment will happen — not in a way that opens a door to its cancellation.

The exit-creating close: *"Okay, so we'll see you Tuesday — and just give us a call if anything changes."*

The commitment-reinforcing close: *"Perfect — we'll see you Tuesday at two. We'll send you a reminder the day before. We're looking forward to it."*

The difference is the phrase *"if anything changes"* — which in the exit-creating close is presented as an obvious possibility, a built-in contingency, an expected outcome. Removing it does not prevent patients from cancelling when they genuinely need to. It simply stops the practice from pre-suggesting cancellation as a natural and expected option.

The Confirmation Call — The Most Misunderstood Conversation in Dentistry

If there is a single communication moment in the dental practice that is more consistently undermined by poor language than any other it is the appointment confirmation call.

Not because practices do not make confirmation calls. Most do. But because the language used in the majority of confirmation calls — however well-intentioned — is doing something the practice never intended.

It is planting the seed of cancellation.

"Hi, this is [Name] from [Practice] calling to confirm your appointment tomorrow at two. Please give us a call if you need to reschedule."

That message — left on voicemail or delivered live dozens of times a day in dental practices across the country — contains two catastrophic communication errors.

The first is the word *"confirm."* To confirm an appointment is to ask the patient to actively affirm that they are still coming — which implicitly raises the possibility that they might not be. It is the verbal equivalent of asking *"you're still planning on doing this, right?"* in a tone that suggests the answer might be no.

The second is the phrase *"if you need to reschedule"* — which pre-builds the exit ramp. It tells the patient, before they have thought about cancelling, exactly how to cancel. It removes friction from the cancellation process at precisely the moment when a small amount of friction — nothing punitive, nothing guilt-inducing, simply the absence of a pre-built off-ramp — would serve the practice's interests.

Now compare that to this:

"Hi [Patient Name], this is [Name] from [Practice]. We're looking forward to seeing you tomorrow at two o'clock. We'll have everything ready for you. See you then!"

No confirmation requested. No reschedule option offered. Simply — warmly, genuinely, briefly — the expression of anticipation and the assumption that the appointment is happening.

That message changes the patient's psychological relationship to the appointment. Instead of being asked whether they are coming — which prompts a mental review of reasons they might not — they are told that someone is looking forward to seeing them. Which prompts a different mental response entirely.

The mental response of someone who is expected.

Research on commitment and consistency — explored extensively by Robert Cialdini and referenced by John Maxwell in his work on influence — shows that people are significantly more likely to follow through on commitments when those commitments are treated as established rather than questioned.

The assumptive confirmation call treats the appointment as established. And established appointments have dramatically lower cancellation rates than questioned ones.

John Maxwell writes:

"Assumptions are the termites of relationships."

The assumption that a patient might cancel — communicated through the language of *"if you need to reschedule"* — is a termite in the appointment commitment. Remove it. Replace it with the assumption of attendance — warm, genuine, and confidently communicated — and watch what happens to the cancellation rate.

Handling the Chronic Re-Scheduler

Every practice has them. The patient who calls — reliably, predictably, almost as though it is their defining characteristic — to move their appointment. Again.

The third reschedule. The fourth. The patient whose name on the schedule is treated as a tentative placeholder rather than a genuine commitment.

The frustrated response — the one that lives in the back of every scheduling coordinator's mind even when it does not reach her lips — is entirely understandable. *"That doesn't work for us."* Or the longer version: *"We've rescheduled this appointment twice already and it's really disruptive to our schedule."*

Both of these responses are honest. Neither of them serves the practice or the patient.

The chronic rescheduler is not, in most cases, a malicious actor deliberately sabotaging the practice's production. They are a person whose life — for reasons that may be entirely invisible to the practice — consistently interferes with their ability to keep dental appointments. Anxiety. Work schedule instability. Family responsibilities. Financial uncertainty about what the visit will cost.

The language that serves this patient — and the practice — addresses the pattern without punishing it:

"I want to make sure we find a time that really works well for you — something that fits your schedule reliably so we can make sure you get the care you need. What tends to be the most consistent time for you?"

That response does three things. It acknowledges the challenge without shaming the patient for it. It redirects the conversation toward a solution — a better time rather than a conversation about the inconvenience of the current situation. And it keeps the focus on the patient's care rather than the practice's frustration.

Sometimes the chronic rescheduler has a logistical problem that a different appointment time genuinely solves. Sometimes they have an anxiety problem that no appointment time solves — and the language that acknowledges their hesitation while gently maintaining the value of their care is the most effective tool available.

"We understand life gets busy — and we really do want to make sure you're able to get in for this. Your care matters to us and we want to make it as easy as possible for you to come in."

Not *"that doesn't work for us."*

Because *"that doesn't work for us"* ends a conversation. And ended conversations do not produce scheduled appointments.

The No-Show Recovery Call

The patient who does not show up for their appointment — who simply is not there when the name is called and the room is prepared and the time is set aside — represents a particular communication challenge.

The natural instinct is to lead with the fact of the absence. *"You missed your appointment today."* Or the gentler but still accusatory: *"We had you scheduled for two o'clock today."*

Both of these openings position the practice as an institution informing a patient of their failure to comply with a commitment. And patients who feel they have been caught failing do not respond with enthusiasm for rescheduling.

They respond with avoidance.

The no-show recovery call that actually works sounds like this:

"Hi [Name], this is [Name] from [Practice]. We missed seeing you today and just wanted to reach out — we hope everything is okay. We'd love to find another time to get you taken care of. Give us a call when you get a chance."

That message does something counter-intuitive. It expresses care for the patient rather than frustration at their absence. It assumes — generously — that something may have prevented them from attending rather than assuming they simply did not bother. And it leaves the door open warmly rather than framing the reschedule as the patient's obligation to repair a wrong.

Patients who receive that message and know they simply forgot — or chose not to come — feel the warmth of the response more acutely because it is more generous than they deserved. And that generosity creates something valuable:

Goodwill.

Goodwill that makes them far more likely to call back, to reschedule, and to show up for the rescheduled appointment with a renewed commitment born partly of gratitude for not being made to feel worse than they already did.

John Maxwell writes:

"Treat people as if they were what they ought to be and you help them to become what they are capable of being."

The no-show recovery call that treats the patient as someone who matters — whose absence was noticed and whose care is still wanted — helps them become the reliable patient they are capable of being. Not through guilt. Through grace.

The Last-Minute Cancellation

The same-day cancellation is the scheduling coordinator's most dreaded call. The appointment that was confirmed. The room that is set up. The provider whose schedule now has a forty-five minute gap that cannot be filled with this much notice.

The response the coordinator wants to give — understandably, humanly, justifiably — is some version of *"you should have called sooner."*

The response that serves the practice — and the patient relationship — is something entirely different:

"Thank you for letting us know. We completely understand. Let's find another time to continue your care — what tends to work well for you?"

Three sentences. The first acknowledges and appreciates the call — because a same-day cancellation call, however inconvenient, is better than a no-show. The second removes any guilt from the interaction. The third immediately moves toward the solution — the rescheduled appointment — rather than dwelling in the problem of the cancellation.

This response does not pretend the cancellation is not inconvenient. It simply chooses not to make the patient pay emotionally for the practice's inconvenience. Because a patient who feels they have been scolded — even gently — for a same-day cancellation does not call back as readily as a patient who felt the cancellation was received with grace.

And calling back is the only outcome that matters in this moment.

The appointment cannot be un-cancelled. The production cannot be recovered today. The only productive question is whether this patient will reschedule — and the language of the cancellation call is the primary determinant of whether the answer is yes.

The Morning Huddle — Scheduling's Most Powerful Tool

Every scheduling and appointment control conversation in this chapter is made more effective — and more consistent — by one daily practice that costs nothing and takes less time than most team members spend checking their phones between patients:

The morning huddle.

Specifically — the morning huddle conducted with a scheduling lens. Not just *"who is coming in today"* but *"what does each patient on today's schedule need from us in order to leave here with their next appointment already scheduled?"*

Because here is the scheduling truth that most practices overlook:

The best time to schedule the next appointment is at the end of the current one.

Not the confirmation call. Not the reactivation call six months later. Not the postcard reminder. The moment when the patient is in the practice — having just received care, feeling the positive outcome of having come in, in relationship with the team that just served them well — is the moment of highest scheduling receptivity.

And the morning huddle is where the team prepares for that moment — identifying which patients are due for hygiene, which have treatment to schedule, which are leaving today without a next appointment and what the specific, warm, non-pressured invitation to schedule will sound like.

"Before you head out today I just want to make sure we get your next visit on the calendar — we want to make sure you're all set for six months from now. Do mornings or afternoons work better for you?"

That is a scheduling invitation. Not a sales pitch. Not a close. A warm, natural, genuinely caring invitation to continue the relationship — made at the moment when the patient is most receptive to making that commitment.

The morning huddle that prepares the team for this moment — specifically, by name, by patient, by the conversation that needs to happen — produces measurably higher same-day scheduling rates than teams that handle these conversations reactively and inconsistently.

John Maxwell on preparation:

"The secret of your success is found in your daily routine."

The daily routine of the morning huddle — conducted with scheduling intentionality — is one of the highest-return investments of time available to any dental practice. Ten minutes of preparation. Appointments filled. Production protected. Patient relationships strengthened.

Every single morning.

The Language of Prime-Time Requests

Every practice has them — the appointment times that every patient wants and that the schedule can only accommodate a fraction of demand for.

After-school slots for pediatric patients. Early morning appointments for professionals. Friday afternoons for patients who have been putting off care and want to minimize time away from work.

The reflexive response to a patient requesting one of these high-demand times — when none are available — is some version of *"we don't have anything at that time."*

Four words. Door closed. Conversation over.

The A.L.I.G.N.™ response to the same situation keeps the door open — by reframing scarcity as value rather than scarcity as limitation:

"Those times are our most requested and they do reserve quickly — but let's look at what we have available and find the best option for you together."

That response does something strategically elegant. It uses the high demand for those appointment times as social proof — other people want these times, which means they are valuable, which means the practice is valuable. It maintains the warmth of the relationship by offering to look together rather than simply reporting the absence of options. And it keeps the patient engaged in the scheduling conversation rather than giving them a reason to disengage.

Most patients, when told that the most requested times reserve quickly, respond with increased flexibility — not because they were manipulated but because scarcity that is communicated with warmth and honesty feels different from the blunt unavailability of *"we don't have anything."*

The language of value-based scarcity is not dishonest. It is accurate — those times do reserve quickly. It is simply choosing to communicate that accuracy in a way that increases rather than decreases the patient's engagement with the scheduling conversation.

Protecting the Schedule as a Cultural Value

The most important thing this chapter can leave the reader with is not a collection of better phrases — though the phrases matter enormously.

It is a shift in how the practice thinks about its schedule.

In most dental practices the schedule is a logistical tool — a grid of time slots to be filled and managed and reported on at the end of the month. It is something that happens to the practice — filling and emptying in response to forces that feel largely outside the practice's control.

In an A.L.I.G.N.™ practice the schedule is a reflection of the practice's communication culture. Every appointment that holds — every patient who shows up on time, ready for their care, committed to the relationship — is a testament to the quality of the scheduling and confirmation conversations that preceded it. Every empty chair is a communication story — a moment where the language did not create enough commitment, enough value, enough connection to survive the ordinary pressures of life between scheduling and arrival.

When the team understands the schedule in those terms — as something they actively shape through the quality of their communication rather than passively manage through logistics — everything changes.

The confirmation call stops being a clerical task and becomes a relationship investment. The scheduling conversation stops being an administrative transaction and becomes a commitment-building moment. The morning huddle stops being a scheduling review and becomes a communication preparation session.

And the schedule — that number every practice owner watches with the intimate anxiety of someone watching their own vital signs — begins to reflect what the practice's communication culture is building every single day.

John Maxwell writes:

"The greatest day in your life and mine is when we take total responsibility for our attitudes. That's the day we truly grow up."

The day a dental practice takes total responsibility for its schedule — recognizing that the language of scheduling is as much within its control as any other system in the practice — is the day the empty chairs begin to fill.

Not because the patients changed.

Because the conversations did.

Chapter Takeaway

The schedule is the heartbeat of the practice — and it is shaped, more than most practices realize, by the language used in scheduling and confirmation conversations. Appointment commitment is not a fixed characteristic of patients — it is a variable influenced directly by how the practice communicates value, anticipation, and the assumption of attendance at every scheduling touchpoint. The A.L.I.G.N.™ approach to scheduling and appointment control is built on five principles: scheduling language that creates commitment rather than exit ramps, confirmation language that assumes attendance rather than questioning it, recovery language that uses grace rather than guilt, and a morning huddle culture that prepares the team for the specific scheduling conversations each day requires. When the practice treats its schedule as a reflection of its communication culture — rather than a logistical tool subject to forces outside its control — the empty chairs begin to fill. Not because the patients changed. Because the conversations did.

What This Means for Your Practice

Case acceptance is the metric I hear about most from practice owners. And it is the metric that is most consistently misdiagnosed.

The typical response to low case acceptance is to look at the treatment presentation itself. All of those things matter. None of them are usually the primary problem.

The primary problem is almost always what happens in the room after the recommendation is made. The pause that gets filled with the wrong language. The hesitation that gets met with apology instead of empathy.

I have watched clinically excellent dentists present clinically excellent treatment plans and lose the case not because the patient did not need the treatment but because the language in the room after the recommendation quietly communicated that the practice was not sure the patient would say yes.

-Here's What I Want You to Remember-

The next time a patient hesitates after a treatment recommendation — resist the instinct to immediately offer a payment plan or reduce the scope.

Instead say this: I want to make sure you have everything you need to feel confident about this. What questions can I answer?

Then wait. Genuinely. For the actual question underneath the hesitation. That question — answered specifically and warmly — closes more treatment plans than any presentation technique available.

Because what the patient needed was not a better explanation. They needed to feel heard first.

Chapter 12

Insurance & Financial Conversations

Money Doesn't Have to Be Awkward — But Only If You Have the Right Language

"A leader is someone who demonstrates what's possible." — John Maxwell

There is a moment that happens in dental practices dozens of times every single day that nobody talks about in dental school, nobody prepares for in team training, and nobody — if they are being completely honest — feels entirely comfortable navigating.

It is the moment when the conversation turns to money.

It happens at the front desk when a patient asks what their insurance will cover. It happens in the treatment coordinator's office when a $4,000 treatment plan lands on the table between a well-meaning team member and a patient who just felt their stomach drop. It happens at checkout when a balance is presented and the patient's face does something complicated — not angry exactly, but not pleased either — and the team member on the other side of the counter wishes desperately that the floor would open up and swallow her.

It happens, in some form, in virtually every patient interaction. And in most practices it is handled with a combination of apologetic energy, clinical detachment, and the kind of verbal hedging that communicates — to the patient receiving it — that the practice itself is not entirely sure this conversation is okay to be having.

That communication lands. And it costs the practice enormously.

Not because patients are unwilling to invest in their oral health. Research consistently shows that patients will invest significantly in dental care when they understand its value, trust the recommendation, and feel that the financial conversation is being handled with confidence and genuine care.

The problem is not the money. It is the conversation about the money.

And the conversation about the money — like every other conversation in A.L.I.G.N.™ — can be transformed by the right language, the right mindset, and the understanding that talking about financial responsibility is not an uncomfortable necessary evil.

It is an act of care.

"The pessimist sees difficulty in every opportunity. The optimist sees the opportunity in every difficulty." — John Maxwell

Why Financial Conversations Feel So Hard

Before we talk about what to say it is worth spending a moment understanding why financial conversations in dental practices feel as difficult as they do — because the discomfort is not random. It has specific, identifiable roots. And understanding those roots makes them easier to address.

Root One — The Healthcare vs. Business Tension.

Dental team members chose their careers because they wanted to help people. The clinical side of that helping feels natural and motivated — it is the reason they are there. The financial side feels like a departure from that purpose — like they are suddenly asked to be something other than a caregiver.

This tension — between the identity of healthcare provider and the reality of running a business that requires payment for its services — creates a subtle but pervasive discomfort in financial conversations that patients sense even when they cannot name it.

The resolution of this tension is not to pretend it does not exist. It is to reframe the financial conversation as an extension of care rather than a departure from it. A practice that is financially healthy can invest in better technology, better continuing education, better team members, and better patient experiences. Collecting appropriate payment for excellent care is not a betrayal of the healthcare mission. It is what makes the healthcare mission sustainable.

When team members genuinely internalize that reframe — when they understand that the financial conversation is part of caring for the patient rather than separate from it — the discomfort begins to dissolve.

Root Two — The Assumption of Patient Resistance.

Many dental team members approach financial conversations with a pre-loaded expectation of resistance. They have had enough difficult financial conversations — enough patients who pushed back, expressed frustration, or declined treatment on financial grounds — that the expectation of difficulty has become the default setting.

And expectation, as any experienced communicator knows, shapes delivery. The team member who approaches a financial conversation expecting resistance communicates that expectation through their tone, their body language, and the subtle defensiveness that creeps into their language before the patient has said a single negative word.

The patient — who may have arrived with no particular resistance at all — picks up on that defensiveness and responds to it. A conversation that might have gone smoothly becomes difficult — not because of the money, but because of the energy that preceded the money conversation.

Root Three — The Absence of Confident Language.

Most dental team members who handle financial conversations were never given specific language for doing so effectively. They were told what information to convey — the fee, the insurance estimate, the patient portion — but never how to convey it in a way that feels confident, warm, and supportive rather than apologetic or transactional.

Into that language vacuum they improvise. And improvised financial language almost always defaults to one of two equally unhelpful modes — either apologetically soft, which communicates that the practice is not sure the fee is justified, or bluntly clinical, which communicates that the practice is not particularly interested in how the patient receives the information.

Neither mode serves the patient. Neither mode serves the practice.

What serves both is the third option — the confident, warm, partnership-oriented financial language that A.L.I.G.N.™ provides.

The Foundation of A.L.I.G.N.™ Financial Language

There are three principles that underlie every financial conversation in an A.L.I.G.N.™ practice. They are not scripts. They are orientations — ways of approaching the financial conversation that shape the language naturally and authentically.

Principle One — Lead with value, not with cost.

Every financial conversation in a dental practice is ultimately a conversation about an exchange — the patient's investment in exchange for the clinical care they receive. The natural human tendency in these conversations is to lead with the cost side of that exchange — to present the number and then defend it.

A.L.I.G.N.™ financial language reverses that sequence. It leads with the value — the clinical benefit, the health protection, the quality of life improvement that the treatment provides — and then connects the investment to that value.

"This treatment is an investment in protecting your long-term oral health — the crown we're placing is designed to strengthen and protect this tooth for many years to come."

That sentence does not hide the fact that money is about to be discussed. It frames the money conversation as a natural extension of the value conversation — so that when the fee is presented it lands in the context of something the patient already understands and values rather than as a standalone number to be evaluated in isolation.

Principle Two — Use partnership language throughout.

The financial conversation is not the practice presenting a bill to a patient. It is two parties working together to find the best path forward for the patient's health — with the practice as the guide and advocate in that process.

Partnership language sounds like:

"Let's look at your options together." "We want to make this as straightforward as possible for you." "Your insurance will contribute toward this — let's look at what that means for your portion." "We have some options that might make this more manageable — shall we go through them?"

The word *"together"* is particularly powerful in financial conversations. It positions the practice and the patient on the same side of the table — looking at the financial reality jointly, with the practice's expertise available to help navigate it — rather than on opposite sides, with the practice presenting a demand and the patient deciding whether to comply.

Principle Three — Confidence without apology.

The financial conversation must be conducted with the same confidence and warmth the practice brings to its clinical communication. Not aggressively. Not without sensitivity to the patient's financial reality. But without the apologetic hedging that communicates uncertainty about whether the practice deserves to be paid for its services.

"Your portion for today's visit is $250" — said calmly, clearly, and warmly — is a confident financial statement. It does not minimize the amount. It does not over-explain it. It presents it as the natural, expected conclusion of the value exchange that just occurred.

Confidence in financial communication is not insensitivity to cost. It is the appropriate self-assurance of a practice that knows its care is worth what it charges — and communicates that assurance in a way that makes the patient more comfortable, not less.

Insurance Language — From Messenger to Advocate

Insurance is the financial conversation that creates the most friction in most dental practices — and it creates that friction primarily because of how it is framed.

In most practices insurance language positions the practice as a passive messenger — the bearer of news from the insurance company that the practice had no role in creating and takes no responsibility for managing.

"Your insurance doesn't cover that." "Insurance won't pay for that." "Your plan doesn't include that."

Every one of these phrases puts the insurance company in the active role — deciding, determining, controlling — and leaves the patient feeling that the practice is simply relaying information rather than advocating for their interests.

The patient hears: *"We tried to help you but the insurance company said no and there is nothing we can do."*

That is not the message a practice committed to patient advocacy wants to send. And it is not accurate — there is almost always something the practice can do, whether it is filing appeals, providing detailed clinical documentation, offering alternative treatment approaches, or helping the patient understand and maximize whatever benefits are available.

A.L.I.G.N.™ insurance language repositions the practice as the patient's advocate — the knowledgeable guide who helps them navigate a complicated system with their interests at the center.

"Your insurance provides an estimated contribution toward this treatment — let me walk you through exactly what that means for your out-of-pocket portion."

Not *"your insurance doesn't cover that"* but *"your insurance contributes toward this."* The shift from *"doesn't cover"* to *"contributes toward"* is small in word count and enormous in patient experience — it moves the conversation from what is missing to what is available.

"Your plan reimburses based on an alternative benefit allowance — let me explain what that means and how we can help you make the most of your coverage."

Not *"insurance downgraded it"* — which sounds like the insurance company did something punitive — but an explanation that gives the patient context and positions the practice as the guide through that context.

"We'll help you maximize any available out-of-network benefits."

Not *"we don't take your insurance"* — which ends the conversation — but an active commitment to helping the patient access whatever value their coverage provides, regardless of network status.

The insurance conversation conducted through an advocacy lens does something that the messenger-based approach cannot:

It keeps the practice on the patient's side.

And patients who feel their practice is on their side do not shop around. They do not leave angry reviews about insurance confusion. They do not blame the practice for limitations that originated with their insurance company.

They trust. And trust — particularly in the confusing, frustrating, inconsistent landscape of dental insurance — is worth more than any network participation status.

The Annual Maximum Conversation

One of the most commonly mishandled insurance conversations in dentistry is the annual maximum — the moment when a patient has utilized most or all of their available insurance benefit for the year and still has treatment that needs to be completed.

The blunt delivery: *"You've maxed out your insurance."*

Two problems with that phrase. The word *"maxed"* carries connotations of excess — as though the patient has done something wrong by using the benefit they pay for. And *"you've maxed out"* positions the insurance limit as a wall rather than a context.

The A.L.I.G.N.™ delivery:

"You've utilized most of your annual benefits — which means you've made great use of your coverage this year. For the remaining treatment let's look at the timing options and financial arrangements that work best for you."

That response does three things. It reframes benefit utilization as a positive — the patient used what they paid for. It acknowledges the remaining treatment without dwelling on the limitation. And it immediately moves toward solutions — timing and financial options — rather than leaving the patient sitting with the feeling of having run out of something.

The patient who leaves that conversation feels helped. The patient who hears *"you've maxed out"* feels stopped.

Both patients have the same insurance reality. Only one of them has a practice that helped them navigate it.

Presenting Large Treatment Plans

There is a specific moment in the financial conversation that every treatment coordinator, every dentist, and every front desk team member who has ever had to present a significant treatment estimate knows intimately.

It is the moment the number lands.

The patient's face does something. Sometimes it is a sharp intake of breath. Sometimes it is a very careful neutrality — the practiced non-reaction of someone who does not want to reveal how significant the number feels. Sometimes it is a direct expression of concern: *"That's a lot more than I expected."*

And in that moment — the moment after the number lands — the language used in the next sixty seconds determines more about the outcome of that treatment presentation than anything that was said before it.

The instinctive response to a patient's financial concern is often either defensive — explaining why the fee is what it is, as though the patient is questioning the practice's integrity — or immediately concessive — moving quickly to discounts or alternatives in a way that inadvertently signals that the original fee was negotiable all along.

Neither response serves the patient or the practice.

The A.L.I.G.N.™ response to the moment the number lands acknowledges the patient's reaction, validates it without amplifying it, and moves immediately into partnership and solutions:

"I completely understand — this is a significant investment. What I'd love to do is walk you through all the options available to you so we can find the path forward that feels most comfortable."

That response does four things in two sentences. It validates the patient's reaction — *"significant investment"* honors the reality of the cost without catastrophizing it. It communicates empathy — *"I completely understand"* — without apology for the fee. It redirects immediately from the number to the options. And the phrase *"path forward"* assumes that there is a path forward — that the treatment will happen, the only question being the route.

From that foundation the financial conversation can explore payment options, timing, phasing of treatment, insurance maximization, and whatever else helps the patient move from the moment of sticker shock to the decision to proceed.

John Maxwell writes:
"The pessimist sees difficulty in every opportunity. The optimist sees opportunity in every difficulty."

The moment the large treatment estimate lands is a difficulty. The A.L.I.G.N.™ financial language sees the opportunity in it — the chance to demonstrate the practice's commitment to the patient's health and its genuine investment in helping them access the care they need.

Financing and Payment Options — Language That Opens Doors

One of the most powerful tools available to a dental practice in the financial conversation is also one of the most consistently under-presented:

Flexible payment and financing options.

Most practices that offer financing — through third-party providers or in-house arrangements — present those options as a last resort. The fee is presented. The patient expresses hesitation. Then, as a kind of rescue operation, the financing option is introduced.

That sequence inadvertently frames financing as something for patients who cannot afford the treatment — which carries its own stigma and which the patient must overcome before they can say yes.

A.L.I.G.N.™ financial language integrates financing into the presentation from the beginning — not as a fallback for patients with financial limitations but as a standard, dignity-preserving option available to any patient who prefers the flexibility of phased payments:

"For a treatment investment at this level we always walk patients through both the full payment option and our flexible payment arrangements — that way you can choose whatever works best for your situation."

That framing does something important. It normalizes the financing option — it is presented as standard rather than remedial. It gives the patient agency — they choose what works best for their situation rather than being offered an alternative because the practice assumed they could not handle the full fee. And it removes the stigma from the conversation entirely — because nobody is being identified as someone who needs financial help. Everyone is simply being offered the options that are always available.

Patients who are offered financing proactively — as a standard option rather than a rescue — accept it more readily and feel better about having done so. And patients who feel good about their financial arrangement are more likely to complete their treatment, more likely to return for future care, and more likely to refer others.

The financial arrangement is part of the patient experience. Make it feel like one.

The Deposit Conversation

For larger or more complex treatments most practices collect a deposit at the time of scheduling — a reasonable practice that protects the practice's time and signals the patient's commitment to moving forward.

How that deposit is requested matters enormously.

The transactional version: *"We require a deposit upfront."*

The word *"require"* frames the deposit as a demand — something the practice extracts from the patient before it will provide service. It is accurate. It is also unnecessarily cold — communicating a transactional relationship rather than a partnership.

The A.L.I.G.N.™ version:

"To reserve this dedicated treatment time for you we collect a scheduling deposit — that ensures this time is held specifically for your care."

That framing changes everything about how the deposit lands. It is not a requirement extracted by the practice. It is the natural mechanism by which the patient's appointment time is specifically reserved — which connects the deposit to the value of reserved, dedicated, personalized care rather than to the practice's financial protection.

Most patients respond to the A.L.I.G.N.™ deposit framing without resistance — because it makes the deposit feel like part of a value exchange rather than a toll at a gate.

When a Patient Says They Cannot Afford It

The patient who says *"I just can't afford it right now"* is not necessarily saying no.

They are often saying: *"I need help finding a way to say yes."*

The response that closes the door: *"I understand — just let us know when you're ready."*

Said kindly. Said with genuine understanding. And heard by the patient as: *"We'll wait, but we're not going to help you figure this out."*

The response that keeps the door open:

"I completely understand — and I want to make sure you have all the information you need to move forward whenever the time is right. Can I share a couple of options that other patients in similar situations have found helpful?"

That response does three things. It validates the patient's reality without accepting it as a permanent barrier. It positions the practice as a resource rather than a waiting room. And the phrase *"whenever the time is right"* communicates patience and continued availability — this is not a one-time offer, and the practice will still be here and still be interested in helping when the patient's situation changes.

Sometimes the patient genuinely cannot afford the treatment today and the right outcome is a warm, respectful conversation that plants the seed of a future yes. Sometimes the patient says they cannot afford it but the real barrier is something else — uncertainty about whether it is necessary, anxiety about the procedure itself, uncertainty about the value — and the language that keeps the door open creates space for that real barrier to surface and be addressed.

Either way — keeping the door open serves the patient's health and the practice's relationship with that patient far better than a polite farewell that closes the conversation entirely.

Dale Carnegie's foundational insight applies here with full force:

"The only way on earth to influence other people is to talk about what they want and show them how to get it."

What the patient who says they cannot afford it wants — almost always — is their health. The financial conversation that keeps talking about what they want — the protection of the tooth, the restoration of function, the elimination of pain, the confidence of a healthy smile — while showing them how to get it within their financial reality is the financial conversation that produces yes.

Not through pressure. Through partnership.

A Word About Discounts

Every practice receives them. The patient who asks directly — *"Is there any kind of discount available?"* — or hints at it — *"That seems like a lot for what it is."*

The reflexive response in many practices is either immediate concession — *"let me see what I can do"* — or flat refusal — *"we don't give discounts."*

Both responses have problems.

Immediate concession devalues the service — implying the original fee was inflated and negotiable, which retroactively damages the patient's trust in the practice's pricing integrity.

Flat refusal closes a door that does not need to be closed — because what the patient asking about a discount often actually needs is not a reduced fee but a better understanding of the value they are receiving or a more flexible payment arrangement.

The A.L.I.G.N.™ response to the discount inquiry:

"What I'd love to do is make sure you have a clear picture of everything that's included in this treatment and walk you through the payment options available to you — I want to make sure we find the best path forward for your situation."

That response acknowledges the patient's financial concern without either conceding on the fee or shutting the conversation down. It redirects toward value — which is almost always the more productive conversation — and toward options — which is almost always the more useful practical response.

A patient who understands the value of what they are receiving and has access to a payment option that fits their budget rarely needs a discount.

A patient who does not understand the value — or does not know their options — will always ask for one.

The Financial Conversation as a Reflection of the Practice's Values

I want to close this chapter with something that goes beyond language technique.

The financial conversation — how a practice handles insurance questions, presents treatment investments, offers payment options, and responds to financial hesitation — is one of the most revealing reflections of the practice's values available to any patient.

A practice that handles financial conversations with confidence, warmth, transparency, and genuine advocacy communicates something about itself that no marketing material can convey:

"We are a practice that respects you. We are transparent about what things cost and why. We are invested in helping you access the care you need. We are on your side even when the conversation is about money."

That communication — felt rather than stated, experienced rather than explained — is one of the most powerful trust-building forces available to any dental practice.

And trust built in the financial conversation — the conversation that most practices approach with the most anxiety and the least preparation — is among the most durable trust available. Because it was built in the hard moment. The vulnerable moment. The moment when the practice could have been transactional and chose instead to be human.

Patients remember that.

They remember it the way they remember every moment when someone treated them better than the situation required.

They remember it — and they come back because of it.

John Maxwell writes:

"People don't care how much you know until they know how much you care."

Nowhere in the dental practice is the truth of that statement more directly tested — or more powerfully validated — than in the financial conversation.

Care enough to have it well.

Chapter Takeaway

Insurance and financial conversations are not a departure from the practice's commitment to patient care — they are an extension of it. The A.L.I.G.N.™ approach to financial communication is built on three principles: lead with value rather than cost, use partnership language that keeps the practice and patient on the same side, and conduct every financial conversation with confidence rather than apology. Insurance language that positions the practice as a patient advocate rather than a passive messenger transforms one of the most friction-filled patient interactions into one of the most trust-building. Financial language that leads with value, integrates options proactively, and responds to hesitation with partnership rather than pressure produces case acceptance rates that reflect the genuine quality of the practice's care — because the financial conversation stops being a barrier and becomes the bridge that carries the patient from the recommendation to the yes.

What This Means for Your Practice

I want to tell you something that took me a long time to say out loud in a coaching session without the room getting uncomfortable.

The financial conversation in most dental practices is being handled apologetically. Not intentionally. Not carelessly. Apologetically.

With the specific tone and the specific language patterns of a team that has absorbed — somewhere in the chain of inherited communication habits — the belief that the fees need to be softened before the patient has said a single word about them.

And that apology — delivered before any objection has been raised, before any concern has been expressed — is the single most damaging communication pattern in the entire patient financial experience.

Because when the practice apologizes for its own value the patient receives that apology as information. If even the practice is not sure this fee is justified — maybe it is not.

-Here's What I Want You to Remember-

Your fees are not the problem. The language around your fees is the problem.

The next financial conversation that happens in your practice — listen for the apology. The hedge. The payment plan offered before the patient has expressed a single concern.

That is where the work begins. And the work — specific, practiced, genuinely achievable — produces a financial conversation that feels like partnership rather than transaction. Every single time.

Chapter 13

Treatment Acceptance & Clinical Communication

The Best Dentistry in the World Doesn't Help If the Patient Says No

"If your actions inspire others to dream more, learn more, do more and become more, you are a leader." — John Maxwell

There is a paradox at the heart of dental practice that nobody in dental school prepares you for.

You can be the most skilled clinician in your city. You can have the most advanced technology, the most accurate diagnoses, the most carefully considered treatment recommendations. You can look at a radiograph and see — with complete clinical certainty — exactly what needs to happen to protect a patient's oral health for the next decade.

And the patient can say no.

Not because your diagnosis is wrong. Not because your recommendation is inappropriate. Not because the patient does not care about their health.

Because the way the recommendation was delivered created a response in the patient that made saying no feel safer than saying yes.

This is the treatment acceptance paradox — and it is playing out in dental practices everywhere, every single day, at enormous cost to patients who are not receiving care they genuinely need and to practices that are not producing what their clinical quality deserves.

The solution is not better clinical skills. The dentist in this scenario already has exceptional clinical skills.

The solution is better clinical communication — the ability to translate clinical excellence into a patient experience that creates understanding, trust, and the confident willingness to say yes to recommended care.

That is what this chapter is about.

"To add value to others, one must first value others." — John Maxwell

Why Patients Say No

Before we talk about what to say let us spend a moment genuinely understanding why patients decline recommended treatment — because the reasons are more varied and more human than most clinical communication approaches acknowledge.

Most dental practices operate on an implicit assumption about treatment declination: patients say no because of cost. And cost is certainly a factor — it would be dishonest to suggest otherwise. But cost alone is rarely the complete story. In practice after practice the patients with the financial means to easily afford recommended treatment decline it at rates that make purely financial explanations insufficient.

The real reasons patients say no are more psychological than financial — and they fall into five consistent categories.

Fear. Not just fear of pain — though that is real and significant — but fear of the unknown. Fear of what the procedure will feel like. Fear of losing control in a clinical environment. Fear of finding out something is worse than they hoped. Clinical language that emphasizes severity and consequence without providing reassurance and a clear path forward activates this fear rather than addressing it.

Skepticism. Particularly in patients who have had negative experiences with dentistry — overtreatment, unexpected costs, recommendations that felt more production-driven than clinically necessary — there is a baseline skepticism about whether recommended treatment is genuinely necessary or commercially motivated. Clinical communication that feels pressured or urgency-based confirms this skepticism rather than dissolving it.

Disconnection from consequence. *"It doesn't hurt"* is the most common objection to treatment acceptance in dentistry — and it is an entirely rational response from a patient whose lived experience tells them that things that do not cause discomfort do not require intervention. Clinical language that fails to bridge the gap between the absence of current symptoms and the presence of a genuine problem leaves patients with no compelling reason to act on a recommendation they cannot feel.

Information overwhelm. The dentist who presents a treatment recommendation with comprehensive clinical detail — because thoroughness feels like responsibility — can inadvertently overwhelm the patient with information they are not equipped to process. A patient who cannot make sense of what they are being told defaults to the safest available response: no.

Lack of connection to personal values. Treatment that is presented purely in clinical terms — what is wrong, what needs to be done, what happens if it is not — fails to connect the recommendation to what the patient actually cares about. Their comfort. Their confidence. Their ability to eat without pain. Their desire to keep their natural teeth for life. Recommendations that speak only to the clinical reality and not to the patient's personal values miss the emotional motivation that makes people act.

Understanding these five reasons changes everything about how clinical communication should be structured. Because the solution to each of them is different — and a communication approach that addresses all five simultaneously is the most powerful treatment acceptance tool available to any clinician.

The Language of Preservation

One of the most significant shifts in clinical communication that A.L.I.G.N.™ produces is the movement from loss language to preservation language.

Loss language focuses on what will happen if the patient does not act:

"You could lose the tooth." "This will get significantly worse." "If we don't treat this now it could affect the surrounding teeth." "You really don't want to let this go."

All of these statements may be clinically accurate. All of them activate the threat response — the neurological state of alarm and defensiveness that makes patients shut down rather than open up. The patient who hears *"you could lose the tooth"* does not hear a clinical recommendation. They hear a threat. And threatened people do not make good decisions. They freeze. They minimize. They say they will think about it.

Preservation language focuses on what the practice is working to protect and maintain:

"Our goal is to strengthen and protect this tooth so it serves you well for many years." "We want to address this now while it's straightforward —

before it becomes a more complex situation." "Protecting the surrounding structure is really important here — and catching this at this stage gives us great options." "We'd love to keep this tooth healthy and strong for you long-term."

Same clinical reality. Completely different emotional experience.

Preservation language does something loss language cannot — it positions the treatment as something being done for the patient rather than to the patient. The recommendation is not about preventing a catastrophe. It is about protecting something the patient values. And people are far more motivated by the prospect of keeping something they value than by the prospect of avoiding something they fear.

John Maxwell speaks to the power of this orientation:

"When you focus on what you have, what you have increases."

Preservation language focuses the patient on what they have — a tooth worth protecting, a smile worth maintaining, an oral health foundation worth investing in. And that focus on value — on what exists and is worth keeping — is a far more powerful motivator than fear of loss.

Connecting Treatment to the Patient's Life

Here is a question that most clinical communication never asks — and that changes treatment acceptance dramatically when it is answered:

What does this patient's oral health actually mean to them personally?

Not in the abstract sense of general health and wellbeing. In the specific, personal, lived sense of what this particular patient cares about in their daily life that their oral health affects.

The executive whose confidence in high-stakes meetings depends partly on her ability to smile without self-consciousness. The grandfather who wants to be able to eat at every family dinner without discomfort. The young professional who knows the appearance of his teeth affects how he presents himself in a competitive industry. The patient who has watched a parent lose teeth and is quietly terrified of the same trajectory.

Every patient has a personal story that makes their oral health matter beyond the clinical. And the clinical communication that connects treatment recommendations to that personal story — that bridges the gap between the diagnosis and the life the patient actually lives — produces treatment acceptance that no amount of clinical detail alone can match.

"You mentioned earlier that you've been having some discomfort when you're eating — placing this crown is going to take that completely off the table and let you enjoy meals without thinking about your teeth. That's a really meaningful quality of life improvement."

"I know confidence in your smile matters to you — and protecting this tooth now is the best way to make sure that stays something you never have to think about."

"You've done such a great job maintaining your teeth over the years — this treatment is really about protecting all that investment and making sure things stay in great shape for you long-term."

These are not manipulative statements. They are empathetic ones — communications that demonstrate the clinician actually listened to what the patient shared about their life and is connecting the clinical recommendation to something that genuinely matters to that specific person.

And they produce yes far more reliably than a clinical summary ever will.

Dale Carnegie — whose insights about human motivation have proven as relevant in the dental operatory as anywhere else — puts it plainly:

"Talk to someone about themselves and they'll listen for hours."

Talk to a patient about their health in the context of their life — their values, their concerns, their personal motivations — and they will not just listen. They will act.

The "It Doesn't Hurt" Conversation

No treatment acceptance challenge is more universal in dentistry — or more consistently mishandled — than the patient who declines recommended treatment because they cannot feel anything wrong.

"It doesn't hurt, so why do I need to fix it?"

This is not an unreasonable question. It is, in fact, an entirely logical question from someone whose experience of their own body tells them that problems hurt and things that do not hurt are not problems.

The instinct of many clinicians is to respond to this question with escalating clinical detail — explaining the pathology in more technical terms, emphasizing the potential severity more strongly, leaning harder on the urgency of the recommendation.

This approach almost never works. It triggers the skepticism and information overwhelm responses described earlier — and often confirms the patient's suspicion that they are being pressured rather than educated.

The A.L.I.G.N.™ response to the *"it doesn't hurt"* objection takes a fundamentally different approach:

"That's actually one of the most important things about catching this now — many dental conditions develop silently, without symptoms, right up until they reach a point where they become much more complex to address. The fact that it doesn't hurt is exactly why this is the ideal time — we have great options right now that we might not have if we wait."

That response validates the patient's observation — *"it doesn't hurt"* is acknowledged as a real and understandable data point rather than dismissed as naivety. It educates without alarming — explaining the silent nature of dental disease progression as useful information rather than a threat. And it reframes the timing — the absence of symptoms is not an argument for inaction. It is an argument for acting now, while the options are still favorable.

The patient who hears that response does not feel pressured. They feel informed. And informed patients — patients who genuinely understand why a recommendation makes sense for their specific situation — say yes at dramatically higher rates than patients who feel they are being told what to do without understanding why.

John Maxwell writes:

"Knowledge is power, but character is what gets things done."

The character dimension of clinical communication — the genuine care for the patient's wellbeing that motivates the recommendation — is what gives the knowledge its power. When patients feel the clinician's genuine investment in their health behind the information they are receiving, the information lands differently.

It lands as advocacy. Not sales.

And advocacy — genuinely felt and authentically communicated — is the most powerful treatment acceptance tool in dentistry.

The Crown Conversation

Of all the treatment recommendations in general dentistry the crown is perhaps the most frequently declined — and the most frequently presented in ways that invite declination.

"You need a crown on this tooth."

Four words. A directive. No context. No explanation of why. No connection to what the patient values. No indication of what the crown protects against or what life looks like after the crown is placed.

The patient hears a significant cost with no compelling narrative around it. The natural response is hesitation — and hesitation, in the absence of a compelling reason to act now, almost always becomes delay.

The A.L.I.G.N.™ crown conversation looks very different:

"What I'm seeing here is that this tooth has developed some stress over time — the kind that happens naturally with years of use. What we'd like to do is place a crown to cover and protect the tooth completely — essentially giving it a strong outer shell that distributes biting force evenly and removes the risk of the tooth fracturing. Our goal is always to protect your natural teeth for as long as possible, and this is the best way to do that for this particular tooth."

That presentation does five things the four-word directive cannot. It normalizes the condition — *"the kind that happens naturally with years of use"* removes blame and reduces alarm. It explains the mechanism of the solution — *"distribute biting force evenly"* gives the patient a mental model of why the crown works. It removes a specific risk — *"removes the risk of fracture"* speaks to protection rather than just treatment. It connects to the patient's long-term interest — *"protect your natural teeth for as long as possible."* And it uses the collaborative *"we"* throughout — *"what we'd like to do"* — which maintains the partnership orientation rather than the directive one.

Presented that way the crown recommendation is not a demand. It is an act of care — clearly explained, specifically connected to the patient's interests, and delivered in the language of preservation rather than loss.

That presentation produces yes.

The Root Canal Reality

If the crown is the most frequently declined routine treatment the root canal is the most feared. The phrase alone carries decades of cultural baggage — the universal shorthand for a painful, dreaded, to-be-avoided-at-all-costs dental experience.

Most of that reputation is obsolete. Modern endodontics — with proper anesthesia and contemporary technique — is not the experience of previous generations. But the cultural association persists. And a clinical communication approach that dismisses that association rather than addressing it directly misses an enormous opportunity to replace fear with reassurance.

The dismissive response: *"It's not that bad."*

Three words that invalidate the patient's fear without providing a single piece of genuinely reassuring information. The patient who hears *"it's not that bad"* does not feel reassured. They feel their concern was not taken seriously. And patients whose concerns are not taken seriously do not open up to the recommendations that follow.

The A.L.I.G.N.™ root canal conversation:

"I completely understand — root canals have a reputation that I think is mostly left over from a very different era of dentistry. What I can tell you is that with the anesthesia and techniques we use today the procedure is actually very manageable — most patients are surprised by how comfortable they feel throughout. Our whole focus is going to be on making sure you're completely numb and completely comfortable before we do anything. And here's the important thing — this is what saves the tooth. Without this treatment the infection will continue to spread and we'd eventually lose the tooth entirely. Saving your natural tooth is always our first goal."

That response does something the dismissive version cannot. It acknowledges the fear — *"I completely understand"* — without amplifying it. It directly addresses the source of the reputation — it is outdated. It provides specific reassurance — the anesthesia, the technique, the focus on comfort. It connects to the patient's value — saving the natural tooth. And it frames the procedure as the positive option — not the thing being done to the patient but the thing that saves something they value.

Fear acknowledged and then educated dissolves far more readily than fear dismissed.

The Hygienist's Voice

Clinical communication in treatment acceptance is not only the domain of the dentist. The hygienist — who spends more time in relationship with most patients than any other clinician in the practice — has an extraordinary and consistently underestimated influence on treatment acceptance.

The hygienist who sees the patient every six months knows their health history, their compliance patterns, their anxieties, and their motivations in a way the dentist — who may spend fifteen minutes with the patient per visit — often cannot. And that knowledge, applied through intentional communication, is one of the most powerful treatment acceptance tools in the practice.

The hygienist who says — in the context of a warm, established, trusting relationship — *"I've been keeping a close eye on this area since your last visit and I do want to make sure Dr. [Name] takes a good look today — I want to make sure we stay ahead of anything before it becomes more complex"* has done something that no amount of in-the-moment clinical persuasion can fully replicate.

She has pre-framed the treatment conversation in the context of an ongoing, caring relationship. The patient who hears that from their hygienist arrives at the treatment presentation having already received a trusted recommendation from someone they have come to rely on.

That context does not guarantee acceptance. But it creates the conditions for it — because the patient is receiving the recommendation as part of a continuous relationship of care rather than as a new piece of information from a clinical authority they may have limited history with.

The hygienist's voice in treatment acceptance is not a secondary influence. In many practices it is the primary one. And investing in the hygienist's communication skills — in her language around diagnosis, treatment recommendation, and patient education — is one of the highest-return clinical communication investments a practice can make.

The Cosmetic Conversation

There is a category of dental treatment that carries its own specific communication challenge — one that is almost the inverse of the challenges we have been discussing.

Cosmetic dentistry.

Unlike restorative and periodontal treatment — where the communication challenge is motivating a patient to act on a clinically necessary recommendation — the cosmetic conversation requires the clinician to validate a patient's desire for elective improvement without the clinical urgency that drives other treatment decisions.

The communication failure in cosmetic conversations often comes from the opposite direction of restorative communication — instead of too much clinical urgency, there is too much clinical dismissal.

"It's only cosmetic."

Said by clinicians who mean to communicate that the procedure is elective — that the patient is not in clinical danger if they choose not to proceed. Said with no negative intention whatsoever. And received by the patient as: *"your desire to feel better about your smile is trivial."*

The patient who has spent years self-conscious about the appearance of their teeth — who smiles with their lips closed in photographs, who catches themselves covering their mouth when they laugh — is not asking for a trivial thing when they inquire about cosmetic treatment. They are asking about something that affects how they move through the world. Their confidence. Their willingness to be fully present in the moments that matter.

That is not trivial. That is profoundly human.

"Feeling genuinely confident in your smile can have a real impact on how you present yourself and how you feel in the moments that matter most to you — whether that's professionally, socially, or just personally. That's not a small thing."

That response validates the emotional significance of the patient's desire without overstating the clinical dimension. It connects the treatment to real life value — the professional presentation, the social confidence, the personal satisfaction. And it communicates that the practice takes the patient's desire seriously — which is the foundation of every cosmetic case acceptance relationship.

Brené Brown writes:

"Daring to set boundaries is about having the courage to love ourselves, even when we risk disappointing others."

Cosmetic dentistry — at its best — is a clinical expression of that principle. It helps patients present themselves as who they genuinely want to be. The communication that honors that aspiration — rather than diminishing it with clinical qualifications — is the communication that builds the cosmetic relationship.

Informed Consent as Communication

Before we close this chapter there is one more dimension of clinical communication worth addressing — one that is typically treated as a legal formality but that is, in its truest form, one of the most powerful trust-building opportunities in the clinical relationship.

Informed consent.

In most practices informed consent is a form. The patient signs it. The procedure proceeds. The consent process is considered complete.

In an A.L.I.G.N.™ practice informed consent is a conversation — a genuine, two-way exchange in which the patient is invited not just to sign off on a procedure but to genuinely understand it, ask questions about it, and confirm their readiness to proceed from a position of real knowledge rather than passive compliance.

"Before we get started I want to make sure you feel completely informed about what we're going to do today and that you feel good about moving forward. Do you have any questions about the procedure or anything you want me to clarify before we begin?"

That question — asked genuinely, with the actual willingness to answer whatever comes up — does something the signed form cannot. It gives the patient control. It communicates that the clinician values their understanding and their comfort more than the efficiency of moving directly to the procedure.

And patients who feel in control — who feel that their understanding was sought and their questions were welcome — are more compliant, more calm, more trusting, and more likely to accept future treatment recommendations.

Informed consent as genuine communication is not a risk management strategy. It is a relationship investment. And the relationship it builds — between a patient who feels genuinely respected and a clinician who demonstrates genuine respect — is the foundation of every treatment acceptance success that follows.

The After-Visit Follow-Up

One of the most underutilized treatment acceptance tools in clinical communication is the follow-up call — the call made one to two days after a procedure to check on the patient's comfort and recovery.

Most practices make follow-up calls when they make them at all as a clinical courtesy — checking for complications, confirming medication effectiveness, ensuring the patient is not experiencing unexpected distress.

All of that is valuable. But the follow-up call does something else that most practices are not intentionally leveraging:

It is the single most powerful producer of positive reviews, referrals, and treatment acceptance for the next recommended procedure in the entire patient experience.

Because nobody calls to check on you.

Not after routine dental procedures. Not in the era of healthcare as transaction. The patient who receives a warm, personal, genuine follow-up call from a member of their dental team — asking not about billing or scheduling but simply *"how are you feeling?"* — experiences something so unexpected and so genuinely caring that it creates an emotional response that outlasts any other aspect of the visit.

"Hi [Name], this is [Name] from [Practice]. I'm just calling to check in and see how you're feeling after your procedure yesterday — is everything comfortable?"

Simple. Thirty seconds. Immeasurably powerful.

The patient who receives that call tells people about it. They mention it in their review. They reference it when recommending the practice to a friend. And when the next treatment recommendation comes — whatever it is, however significant the investment — they say yes more readily than any other patient in the practice.

Because a practice that calls to check on you after a procedure is a practice that has proved it cares about you specifically.

And people say yes to places that care about them specifically.

John Maxwell writes:

"People don't care how much you know until they know how much you care."

The follow-up call is thirty seconds of demonstrating how much you care.

It is worth more than any case presentation technique ever devised.

Chapter Takeaway

Treatment acceptance is not a closing skill — it is a communication skill. Patients decline treatment not primarily because of cost but because of fear, skepticism, disconnection from consequence, information overwhelm, or failure to connect the recommendation to their personal values. A.L.I.G.N.™ clinical communication addresses all five of these barriers through preservation language that focuses on protecting what the patient values rather than warning of what they might lose, personal connection language that bridges the diagnosis to the patient's actual life, validation-first responses to the most common objections, and the follow-up communication that turns a single procedure into a lasting relationship of trust. The best dentistry in the world does not help if the patient says no. The best clinical communication ensures that the patient has every reason — emotional, informational, relational — to say yes.

What This Means for Your Practice

The confirmation call is the most underestimated communication tool in the dental practice.

Not because it is complicated. Because nobody has ever fully examined what the language of the confirmation call is actually communicating to the patient on the other end of it.

Are you still planning on coming in tomorrow?

I have heard that phrase — or some version of it — in virtually every dental practice I have ever worked with. And every time I hear it I think the same thing.

That phrase just gave the patient permission to reconsider.

Not maliciously. The team member who said it was trying to confirm the appointment. What they actually did — through the word still and the word planning — was plant the seed of doubt in a patient who had not previously considered changing their appointment.

-Here's What I Want You to Remember-

Replace every questioning confirmation call with an assumptive one this week.

Not are you still coming — but we are looking forward to seeing you tomorrow at two o'clock. Is there anything you need from us before your appointment?

Run that language for two weeks and track your cancellation rate. The number will tell you everything you need to know about what the old language was actually doing.

Chapter 14

Reactivation, Retention & Team Leadership

The Patients You Already Have Are Your Greatest Growth Opportunity

"The secret to success is to do the common things uncommonly well." — John Maxwell

There is a goldmine in your practice right now.

It is not in your marketing budget. It is not in your new patient pipeline. It is not in the latest technology acquisition or the expanded service offering or the social media strategy your front desk coordinator has been suggesting for the past six months.

It is in your patient database.

Specifically — it is in the names that have gone quiet. The patients who came in once or twice or regularly for years and then simply stopped appearing on the schedule. The patients with diagnosed but unscheduled treatment sitting in their chart. The patients who are three months overdue for hygiene, or six months, or two years. The patients who called once with a question and were never followed up with. The patients who cancelled and were not rescheduled before they fell into the gap between intention and inaction.

In the average dental practice that database represents hundreds of thousands of dollars in immediately accessible production — production that does not require a single new patient acquisition, a single marketing dollar, or a single new service offering to unlock.

It requires only one thing:

The right conversation.

Specifically — the right words, in the right tone, at the right moment, from a place of genuine care rather than administrative obligation.

That is the reactivation opportunity. And it is larger, more immediate, and more relationship-preserving than almost any other growth lever available to a dental practice.

But it is also one of the most consistently mishandled communication categories in dentistry — because the language most practices use in reactivation outreach does precisely the opposite of what is needed. Instead of opening the door it closes it. Instead of creating connection it creates shame. Instead of inviting the patient back it confirms every reason they have been staying away.

This chapter is about fixing that — permanently.

"You can make more friends in two months by becoming interested in other people than you can in two years by trying to get other people interested in you." — Dale Carnegie, cited in John Maxwell's leadership work

Why Patients Go Quiet

Before we address how to bring patients back it is worth understanding why they left — or more accurately, why they drifted.

Because most patient attrition in dental practices is not dramatic. Patients do not typically storm out after a bad experience and announce they are never returning. They simply — gradually, quietly, without fanfare — stop coming.

The reasons are as varied as the patients themselves. Life got busy. Insurance changed. The co-pay felt like a lower priority than the other financial demands of a particular season. A team member they loved left and the practice felt slightly less familiar without her. They had an appointment that felt rushed or impersonal and the motivation to reschedule never quite materialized. They meant to call back but the weeks became months and the months became a year and by then the gap itself felt like a barrier.

None of these are dramatic. None of them are irreversible. And almost none of them are genuine rejections of the practice or its care.

They are the ordinary drifting of human beings moving through busy lives — and the practice that reaches out with warmth, without judgment, and with genuine interest in the patient's wellbeing has an extraordinarily high success rate at bringing those patients back.

The practice that reaches out with the language of obligation and overdue accountability has a significantly lower one.

John Maxwell writes:

"People don't care about your problems. They care about their own."

The reactivation call that leads with the practice's problem — the overdue hygiene appointment, the unscheduled treatment, the gap in the schedule — is a call about the practice's needs. Patients do not respond enthusiastically to calls about someone else's needs.

The reactivation call that leads with the patient's interests — their health, their comfort, their continued wellbeing — is a call about them. And people respond to calls about them.

The Reactivation Call — What Not to Say

Let us start here — with the language that most reactivation calls use and that most consistently produces the outcome practices least want.

"Hi, this is [Name] from [Practice]. You're overdue for your cleaning."

That sentence — or some variation of it — is the opening of reactivation calls in dental practices across the country. Every single day. And it is costing those practices patients they could have kept.

Here is what the patient hears when they hear *"you're overdue."*

They hear an accusation. They hear that they have failed to meet an obligation. They hear the implicit judgment of an institution telling them they have done something wrong. And they respond — emotionally, automatically, entirely predictably — with defensiveness.

Defensiveness does not produce scheduled appointments. It produces excuses, avoidance, and the quiet decision to continue staying away rather than return to a place that makes them feel bad about themselves.

The patient who has not been in for two years knows they have not been in for two years. They do not need the information. They need the welcome.

Other reactivation language patterns to avoid:

"You still haven't scheduled that treatment we recommended." — Accusatory. Implies neglect.

"We've been trying to reach you." — Mildly aggressive. Creates guilt without connection.

"Your account shows you haven't been in since..." — Clinical and cold. Positions the patient as a record rather than a person.

"You need to come in soon." — Directive without relationship. Tells the patient what to do without expressing genuine care about why it matters for them specifically.

Every one of these openings creates an emotional barrier between the practice and the patient before the conversation has had a chance to become one. And once a barrier is up in a reactivation call it is almost never successfully dismantled in the same conversation.

The Reactivation Call — What to Say Instead

The A.L.I.G.N.™ reactivation call is built on a single foundational principle:

Lead with care. Every time. Without exception.

Not care as a technique. Not care as a sales approach. Genuine, specific, personal care for this patient's health and wellbeing — communicated in language that makes the patient feel remembered, valued, and welcomed rather than overdue, delinquent, or obligated.

"Hi [Name], this is [Name] from [Practice]. We've been thinking about you and just wanted to reach out to see how you're doing and make sure you're taken care of."

That opening does three things in one sentence. It communicates that the patient was specifically remembered — *"we've been thinking about you"* is a human statement, not an administrative one. It expresses genuine interest in their wellbeing — *"see how you're doing."* And it offers care — *"make sure you're taken care of"* — rather than demanding compliance.

The patient who receives that call does not feel accused. They feel remembered. And feeling remembered — particularly by a healthcare provider in an era of impersonal institutional healthcare — is both surprising and powerful.

From that warm opening the conversation can naturally move toward care:

"We noticed it's been a little while since we've seen you and we'd love to get you back in — is there a time in the coming weeks that might work well for you?"

Note what is not in that sentence. There is no mention of how long it has been. There is no reference to the specific number of months or years of absence. There is simply — *"it's been a little while"* — an acknowledgment without dwelling, followed immediately by the forward-looking invitation.

The patient who has been avoiding the call because they were braced for judgment receives something entirely different. They receive an invitation. And invitations — offered warmly and without condition — are remarkably difficult to decline.

Following Up on Unscheduled Treatment

The follow-up call for unscheduled treatment — treatment that has been diagnosed, presented, and declined or deferred — requires a slightly different approach from the general reactivation call.

The patient in this scenario has already had the treatment conversation. They said no — or more often they said *"let me think about it"* — and then did not call back. And now the practice is reaching out to revisit a conversation the patient may have hoped was behind them.

The language that re-opens this conversation matters enormously — because it determines whether the patient feels pursued or supported.

"Hi [Name], this is [Name] from [Practice]. I just wanted to follow up and see if you had any questions about the treatment Dr. [Name] recommended at your last visit. We want to make sure you have everything you need to feel comfortable moving forward whenever the time is right for you."

That message does several important things. It frames the call as informational support — *"see if you had any questions"* — rather than as pressure to schedule. It communicates patience and respect for the patient's timeline — *"whenever the time is right for you."* And it positions the practice as a resource rather than a creditor — available to help, not pursuing a transaction.

The patient who receives that call and had genuine questions — but did not know how to ask them without feeling pressure — now has an opening. The patient who had concerns about cost has a natural opportunity to raise them. The patient who was simply not ready but is now closer to readiness has a warm re-entry point.

And the patient who is still not ready hears — in the language of the call — that the practice respects that. Which keeps the relationship intact for the conversation that will eventually move them to yes.

John Maxwell writes:

"Patience is not the ability to wait but the ability to keep a good attitude while waiting."

The follow-up call done right is an expression of exactly that patience — continued care, continued availability, continued genuine interest in the patient's wellbeing, offered without pressure and without judgment.

That patience — communicated consistently — is what eventually produces yes.

Patient Retention — The Language of Loyalty

Reactivation addresses the patients who have already drifted. Retention is the work of ensuring they never drift in the first place.

And retention — the quiet, steady, year-over-year maintenance of the patient relationships a practice has worked so hard to build — is driven by something simpler and more powerful than any loyalty program or recall system a practice could implement.

It is driven by how patients feel every time they interact with the practice.

Not every visit will be remarkable. Not every appointment will produce a memorable moment of extraordinary care. Most dental appointments are routine — and routine, by definition, does not stand out.

What stands out — what creates the cumulative experience that makes patients stay — is the consistent feeling that this practice sees them as a person. That their name is known. That their history is remembered. That their comfort and their experience matter to the team that cares for them.

That feeling is created — or destroyed — in the small moments that nobody thinks of as retention investments but that are, in fact, the most powerful ones:

The team member who remembers that a patient mentioned their child's school play at the last visit and asks how it went. The hygienist who recalls that a patient was anxious last time and proactively addresses it before it becomes visible. The dentist who takes thirty seconds after a procedure to check in personally — not clinically, personally. The front desk coordinator who uses the patient's name twice in a two-minute checkout conversation.

None of these cost money. None of them require new systems or additional staff or a technology investment.

They require only attention — the genuine, specific, person-to-person attention that communicates: *you matter here. Not as a patient. As a person.*

And people who feel that they matter — specifically and personally — do not leave.

They stay. They refer. They write the reviews that begin with *"I actually look forward to going to the dentist"* — a sentence that no marketing campaign in history has ever produced but that the right practice culture produces regularly.

The Checkout Conversation

One of the most overlooked retention moments in the entire patient experience is the checkout conversation — the final interaction of every visit that most practices handle as a purely administrative transaction.

Payment collected. Next appointment scheduled. Receipt printed. Goodbye.

Efficient. Impersonal. A missed opportunity of significant proportions.

The checkout conversation is the last emotional impression of the visit — and last impressions, like first impressions, carry disproportionate weight in how the overall experience is remembered and described.

A checkout conversation that ends warmly — that leaves the patient feeling specifically valued and genuinely anticipated at their next visit — sends them into their day carrying the positive residue of the experience. A checkout conversation that ends transactionally sends them into their day carrying nothing of significance — and nothing of significance is not a neutral outcome. It is the absence of the connection that retention depends on.

The A.L.I.G.N.™ checkout conversation has three elements.

The clinical affirmation. A brief, warm, specific acknowledgment of what happened today and why it matters.

"Everything looks really great — Dr. [Name] is really pleased with how things are progressing. You're doing a great job taking care of your teeth."

Not generic praise. Specific, genuine acknowledgment that communicates the team noticed something worth noting.

The forward connection. The natural, warm scheduling of the next appointment — framed not as a logistical necessity but as the continuation of an ongoing relationship.

"Let's get your next visit on the calendar — we want to make sure you're all set for six months from now. Do mornings or afternoons tend to work best?"

Not *"do you want to schedule your next appointment"* — which invites a no — but the assumptive, warm movement toward the next visit as a natural continuation of care.

The genuine farewell. Not a transactional goodbye. A warm, specific, personal send-off.

"It was great to see you today — we'll look forward to seeing you in [month]. Take care of yourself."

Thirty seconds. The patient leaves feeling valued. The appointment is on the books. The retention investment was made.

Every. Single. Visit.

Team Leadership Communication — The Final Frontier

We have spent the majority of this book talking about how dental teams communicate with patients. But there is a communication dimension that is equally critical to practice success — and that most practice management conversations address either superficially or not at all.

How leaders communicate with their teams.

Because here is the truth that every chapter of this book has been building toward:

A team cannot consistently communicate care to patients that they do not consistently receive from their leaders.

It is not possible to create an externally warm, patient-centered, trust-building communication culture in a practice whose internal culture is driven by pressure, judgment, or the daily experience of being managed rather than led.

The team member who spends her day feeling seen, supported, coached, and genuinely valued by her leadership communicates something different to patients than the team member who spends her day feeling criticized, overlooked, or like a performance metric with a name badge.

Patients feel the difference. It shows in tone. In energy. In the quality of presence that a team member brings to patient interactions when they love their work versus when they are simply enduring it.

Leadership communication is patient communication — one generation removed.

John Maxwell has dedicated his career to this truth:

"The function of leadership is to produce more leaders, not more followers."

The leadership communication that A.L.I.G.N.™ cultivates is not the communication of a manager directing compliance. It is the communication of a leader developing people — treating every team interaction as an opportunity to build someone's confidence, clarify their purpose, and invest in their growth.

When a Team Member Makes a Mistake

The moment that most clearly reveals a leader's communication culture — and that most directly shapes the team's communication with patients — is the moment when something goes wrong.

A scheduling error. A miscommunication with a patient. A missed responsibility. A procedure that did not go as planned.

These moments happen in every practice. They are not indicators of a bad team. They are the inevitable reality of a busy, human, imperfect clinical environment. What matters — what shapes the culture more than any other single factor — is not that mistakes happen but how leadership responds when they do.

The response that damages culture:
"You dropped the ball. This cannot happen again."

Said with frustration. Said with the implicit message that the team member's value is contingent on their error rate. Said in a way that the team member will remember long after the specific mistake has been forgotten — not for the correction it provided but for the shame it created.

Shame does not produce better performance. It produces self-protection. And team members in self-protection mode do not take the creative risks, the communicative initiative, and the genuine patient investment that the best dental practices depend on.

The response that builds culture:

"Let's talk about what happened and figure out together how we handle this differently next time."

That response does something the shame-based response cannot. It treats the mistake as information rather than character evidence. It maintains the relationship between leader and team member — *"together"* is one of the most powerful words in leadership communication. And it focuses on the future rather than dwelling in the past — *"how we handle this differently next time"* assumes the team member will have a next time, which communicates confidence in their fundamental reliability.

John Maxwell is direct about this:

"Great leaders are almost always great simplifiers, who can cut through argument, debate and doubt to offer a solution everybody can understand."

The leader who models that generosity in the mistake moments creates a team that mirrors that generosity in the difficult patient moments. The team that has been treated with grace when they failed is the team most capable of extending grace to the patient who arrives late, forgets their paperwork, or pushes back on a treatment recommendation.

Grace flows from the top.

Make sure there is enough of it there to reach every patient who walks through the door.

The Morning Huddle as a Leadership Communication Tool

We have discussed the morning huddle extensively throughout this book — as an awareness tool, as a scheduling preparation vehicle, as a language reinforcement mechanism. But it is worth addressing it one final time in its most fundamental dimension:

As the daily expression of a leader's communication values.

The morning huddle is the single moment in every practice day when the leader has the full team's attention — when the tone they set, the energy they bring, and the language they model will ripple through every patient interaction that follows.

A leader who comes to the huddle rushed, distracted, and purely logistical communicates — without saying it explicitly — that the day is about getting through. About production. About management.

A leader who comes to the huddle present, energized, and genuinely invested in the team's preparation communicates something entirely different. That the day is about something meaningful. That the people in the room matter. That what happens in the next eight hours with the patients who walk through the door is worth being intentional about.

"Good morning — let's take a few minutes to talk about who we're serving today and how we want them to feel when they leave."

That sentence — or something like it — sets a completely different emotional temperature for the day than *"okay, let's go through the schedule."*

Same information. Entirely different culture.

John Maxwell writes:

"The quality of a leader is reflected in the standards they set for themselves."

The morning huddle is where a leader shows the way — every morning, without exception, in full view of the team they are asking to follow.

Make it count.

Staff Retention as a Communication Outcome

One final dimension of team leadership communication deserves specific attention — because it connects the internal culture of the practice directly to one of the most significant operational and financial challenges in modern dentistry.

Staff retention.

The dental industry faces a staffing challenge that is well-documented and widely discussed — high turnover rates, difficulty recruiting qualified team members, the significant financial and cultural cost of frequent transitions. Practices spend enormous energy and resources on recruiting, hiring, and onboarding new team members — energy that could be invested in growth if the team members they already have chose to stay.

The research on why dental team members leave is consistent and largely unsurprising.

They leave because of culture. Because of how they are treated. Because of the daily communication experience of working in a practice where they feel like a resource rather than a person. Where their concerns are not heard. Where their growth is not invested in. Where the language of leadership is directive rather than developmental.

And they stay — the good ones, the ones whose institutional knowledge and patient relationships represent enormous value to the practice — where the opposite is true. Where they feel seen. Where their contributions are recognized specifically and genuinely. Where the leadership communicates consistent care for their development and their wellbeing.

Staff retention is not a human resources problem. It is a communication problem. And it is one that A.L.I.G.N.™ leadership communication addresses directly — by building the daily language habits of recognition, coaching, transparency, and genuine investment that make good team members feel valued enough to stay.

The practice that retains its best people for five, seven, ten years or more has a competitive advantage that no new hire can provide — the depth of relationship, the clinical consistency, the patient loyalty, and the cultural stability that only time and trust can build.

That advantage is built one leadership conversation at a time.

John Maxwell captures the long-term vision of this work with words that serve as a fitting close to this chapter:

"The greatest gift you can give someone is the gift of your time and attention."

Give it to your team. Every day. In the morning huddle. In the hallway conversation. In the coaching moment. In the recognition that takes thirty seconds and creates loyalty that lasts years.

Give it to your patients. In the reactivation call that leads with care. In the checkout conversation that ends with warmth. In the follow-up call that nobody else makes but that your practice makes every time.

Give it — consistently, intentionally, and generously — and the practice that results will be something that neither a marketing campaign nor a production target nor a management system could ever build on its own.

It will be a practice built on relationships.

And relationships — genuine, well-tended, consistently communicated relationships — are the only foundation in dentistry that never needs replacing.

Chapter Takeaway

The patients already in a practice's database represent its greatest and most immediately accessible growth opportunity — but only if the language used to reach them leads with care rather than obligation. Reactivation calls that open with genuine interest in the patient's wellbeing produce dramatically higher scheduling rates than calls that lead with overdue notices or administrative reminders. Retention is built in the small moments of every visit — the specific acknowledgment, the remembered detail, the warm checkout conversation — that accumulate over time into the feeling of being genuinely valued. And team leadership communication — how leaders respond to mistakes, how they conduct the morning huddle, how they invest in their team members' development — is the foundation on which the entire patient communication culture rests. A team that is led with grace communicates with grace. A team that is developed with intentionality communicates with intentionality. The patients feel it. The metrics reflect it. And the practice that builds both its patient relationships and its team relationships on the A.L.I.G.N.™ communication principles does not just grow — it thrives, sustainably, in a way that compounds with every passing year.

What This Means for Your Practice

The lapsed patient list in most dental practices represents one of the largest untapped revenue opportunities available — and one of the most consistently mishandled communication situations I encounter.

Not because the practices do not want those patients back. But because the language being used to invite them back is doing the opposite of what the practice intends.

Our records show you are overdue for your preventive care appointment.

I want you to sit with that sentence for a moment and experience it as the patient receiving it. You are overdue.

-Here's What I Want You to Remember-

That phrase does not create motivation. It creates shame. And shame — as a communication strategy for reconnecting with a patient who has drifted away — produces avoidance rather than action.

Every patient on your lapsed list is a person — not a production opportunity. They left for reasons that may have had nothing to do with your practice.

Call them like you are genuinely glad they exist. Ask how they are. Not how long it has been since their last cleaning.

Because patients do not return to the practice that reminded them they were overdue.

They return to the practice that made them feel missed.

Chapter 15

The Practice That A.L.I.G.N.s

What Changes When the Whole System Works

"Alone we can do so little; together we can do so much." — Aristotle, cited frequently by John Maxwell

It is a Tuesday morning in a dental practice that has been through the A.L.I.G.N.™ process.

Not a fictional practice. Not an idealized version of something that exists only in the imagination of a practice management consultant. A real practice — with real scheduling pressures and real insurance frustrations and real team members who have good days and difficult ones and real patients who arrive late and cancel and push back on treatment recommendations and sometimes make the front desk coordinator close her eyes briefly and take a breath before she picks up the phone again.

A real practice. Doing real work. In a real world that does not always cooperate with best intentions.

But a practice that communicates differently than it did eighteen months ago. A practice whose team members reach for different words now — not because they are performing a script but because the principles behind those words have become genuinely theirs. A practice whose culture is visible to every patient who walks through the door, audible on every phone call, and felt in every interaction from the first hello to the final goodbye.

Let us spend a morning there.

"The secret of your success is found in your daily routine." — John Maxwell

7:45 AM — The Morning Huddle

The team gathers before the first patient arrives. Not rushed. Not distracted. Present.

The office manager — who has been with the practice for nine years and who has led this huddle for the past fourteen months with a consistency that has become one of the cultural anchors of the practice — opens the same way she opens every huddle:

"Good morning. Let's talk about who we're serving today and how we want them to feel when they leave."

Twelve words. The entire philosophy of A.L.I.G.N.™ in a single sentence.

The team goes through the schedule — not as a logistical exercise but as a communication preparation. Three new patients today. One of them mentioned on the intake form that she has significant dental anxiety. The team notes her name. The hygienist who will see her first knows to open with acknowledgment rather than procedure. The front desk coordinator knows to greet her with particular warmth when she arrives — to make the waiting room feel less clinical, more welcoming, before the clinical interaction begins.

There is a patient at 10:30 with unscheduled treatment from his last visit — a crown recommendation he deferred six weeks ago. Dr. [Name] and the treatment coordinator spend ninety seconds discussing the language approach. Not a script. A strategy. Lead with preservation. Connect it to his stated concern about keeping his natural teeth. Create the space for questions before assuming he has made a final decision.

There is a reactivation call to make today — a patient who has not been in for eighteen months. The scheduling coordinator has already prepared her approach. Not *"you're overdue." "We've been thinking about you."*

The huddle closes the way it always closes — with the question the office manager asks every morning:

"What do we want our patients to walk out saying about us today?"

The answers from the team are not scripted. They are genuine — and they vary slightly from person to person in a way that reflects individual personalities rather than uniform compliance. But they orbit the same gravitational center:

That they were cared for. That they felt like people, not patients. That they walked out knowing they called the right place.

Eight minutes. The day begins.

8:05 AM — The First Call

The phone rings before the first patient has arrived. A woman's voice — slightly tentative, the particular quality of someone who has been putting off making this call and has finally decided to make it.

"Hi — I was wondering if you're taking new patients?"

The scheduling coordinator — the same woman who, fourteen months ago, would have answered this call while simultaneously checking the schedule and mentally composing a response to an email — is fully present for this call. It is the first call of the day. She treats it that way.

"We absolutely are — and we'd love to have you. Can I ask what's bringing you to us today?"

A discovery question. Genuine interest. Not *"what insurance do you have"* — though that will come — but *"what's bringing you to us."* A question that treats the caller as a person with a story rather than an inquiry to be processed.

The woman explains. She has not been to a dentist in almost three years. She knows she needs to go. She has been anxious about it — nothing specific, just a general unease about dental offices that she has carried since childhood.

"I'm really glad you called. A lot of our patients feel the same way when they first reach out to us — and I can tell you that making their experience as comfortable as possible is something our whole team takes really seriously. Can I tell you a little about what your first visit would look like?"

She does. Not a sales pitch. An education — warm, specific, reassuring. What will happen at the first visit. How long it takes. What the doctor is like. What the team does specifically for patients who have some anxiety about dental care.

By the end of the conversation the woman is not just scheduled. She is genuinely looking forward to coming in. She mentions — unprompted — that she has already told her husband about the practice.

She has not been a patient for five minutes and she has made her first referral.

The scheduling coordinator puts down the phone. She does not know this. She will never know this particular story. She simply picks up the next call.

That is what consistent communication culture produces. Outcomes that nobody can see in the moment but that compound invisibly in the background of every conversation.

9:15 AM — The Anxious Patient Arrives

Her name is on the schedule. The team knows it. The front desk coordinator sees her push open the door — a woman in her mid-forties, slight hesitation in her step, the particular quality of someone who has decided to be brave about something that does not feel entirely comfortable.

"Good morning — are you Sarah? We've been looking forward to meeting you. Welcome."

The woman stops. Just for a moment. The greeting surprised her — not dramatically, but perceptibly. She was braced for a clipboard and a waiting room.

She received a welcome.

The difference is not enormous in objective terms. It is enormous in experiential ones. Her nervous system — which arrived primed for the experience of dental anxiety — receives a different signal than it expected. The signal is: *you are safe here.*

When the hygienist calls her back she does something that takes approximately forty-five additional seconds but that changes the entire trajectory of the appointment:

She sits down across from Sarah before the appointment begins. Not in a clinical position. In a conversational one.

"Before we get started I just want to check in — I know coming in can feel a little stressful sometimes, especially if it's been a while. Is there anything I can do to make this more comfortable for you today? You are completely in control — if you need me to slow down or stop at any point just raise your hand and I will."

The woman — who has been holding a small amount of tension in her shoulders since she arrived — exhales.

"I just — I always feel kind of silly about it. I know it's not a big deal."

"It's not silly at all. A lot of people feel exactly the same way. Your feelings are completely valid and we're going to take really good care of you."

Forty-five seconds. The appointment proceeds — without incident, without drama — and concludes with something that does not happen in the majority of dental offices in the country:

The patient, at checkout, says: *"That was actually fine. That was really fine. Can I make my next appointment now?"*

She does.

10:30 AM — The Unscheduled Treatment Conversation

The patient at 10:30 — the one with the deferred crown recommendation — arrives on time. He has been a patient for four years. He is a good patient — consistent, generally compliant, genuinely engaged with his oral health. The crown recommendation surprised him six weeks ago and he asked for time to think about it.

He has not called.

After his hygiene appointment Dr. [Name] comes in — not with the energy of someone revisiting a declined recommendation, but with the genuine warmth of a clinician who is interested in where this patient is.

"How are you feeling about the conversation we had last time about tooth fourteen? I know you wanted some time to think about it — do you have any questions I can answer?"

Not *"have you made a decision."* Not *"are you ready to schedule."* Simply — are there questions? Is there anything in the way of clarity that I can provide?

The patient has a question. Two, actually. One about the procedure itself — how long it takes, whether it will be uncomfortable. One about timing

— he has a busy travel schedule in the next six weeks and wonders whether waiting matters.

Dr. [Name] answers both. Honestly. Without urgency. Without pressure.

On the timing question — the honest clinical answer is that six more weeks is unlikely to create a significantly different clinical situation, but that the longer the tooth is under stress without protection the less predictable the outcome. Not *"if you wait you could lose the tooth."* The honest, specific, preservation-oriented truth about what the timing means clinically.

The patient nods. He understands. He asks one more question — about the cost, specifically about whether his insurance will cover any of it.

The treatment coordinator steps in with the same confident, advocacy-oriented financial language that this practice uses for every financial conversation. She walks him through his estimated insurance contribution. She walks him through the patient portion. She offers the flexible payment arrangement as a standard option — not a rescue, just an option.

The patient schedules the crown.

He does not feel pressured. He does not feel like something was done to him. He feels — accurately — that a practice he trusts spent thirty minutes helping him understand something about his health and then supported him in making a good decision for himself.

That is treatment acceptance when it works the way it is supposed to.

11:45 AM — The Reactivation Call

In a brief window between morning patients the scheduling coordinator makes the reactivation call she prepared for in this morning's huddle.

She dials. The phone rings three times. A man answers — slightly guarded, the particular quality of someone who recognizes the area code and is mildly braced for whatever is about to be asked of him.

"Hi — is this Michael? This is [Name] from [Practice]. We've been thinking about you and just wanted to reach out to see how you're doing."

A pause. The guardedness shifts — slightly, perceptibly.

"Oh — I'm good. Yeah, I know it's been a while. I kept meaning to call."

"No need to explain at all — we're just glad you're doing well. We'd love to get you back in whenever the time is right for you. Is there a time in the coming few weeks that might work?"

Not *"you're eighteen months overdue."* Not *"you have unscheduled treatment on your chart."* Not *"we've been trying to reach you."*

Just — we've been thinking about you. We're glad you're well. We'd love to see you.

Michael schedules an appointment. Not because he was guilted into it. Not because the scheduling coordinator deployed a technique. Because a practice he had been mildly avoiding reached out in a way that made coming back feel easy rather than difficult.

He mentions — before he hangs up — that he has been meaning to bring his wife in as a new patient.

Another referral. From a reactivation call. In a practice that leads with care.

2:30 PM — A Difficult Moment

Not everything in an A.L.I.G.N.™ practice goes perfectly. That is not what this chapter is claiming.

At 2:30 a patient arrives frustrated. He received an explanation of benefits from his insurance company that does not match what he expected to pay based on a conversation with the front desk three weeks ago. The discrepancy is not enormous — but it is real, and he has arrived with the particular energy of someone who feels he was misled.

The front desk coordinator who greets him — the same coordinator who has been with the practice for six years and whose communication has been transformed by the A.L.I.G.N.™ process — does not become defensive. She does not explain immediately. She does not justify.

She listens. Fully. Without interruption. Until the patient has said everything he needs to say.

"I completely understand your frustration — and I'm really glad you came in so we can look at this together. Let me pull up exactly what was discussed and compare it with what the insurance sent — I want to make sure we get to the bottom of this for you."

No blame. No defensiveness. No transfer of responsibility to the insurance company before the facts are even reviewed.

The issue, when examined, turns out to be an insurance processing anomaly — not an error in what the front desk communicated. But the process of reviewing it together — with the practice functioning as the patient's advocate rather than defending its own position — produces something that the correct answer alone never could:

Trust.

The patient leaves satisfied — not because the problem never happened but because of how the practice responded when it did. He will remember this moment. Not as a negative — as a proof.

A proof that this is a practice that stands behind its patients even when the conversation is uncomfortable.

That is A.L.I.G.N.™ culture under pressure. And culture under pressure is the only culture worth having.

4:45 PM — The Last Appointment

The last patient of the day checks out at 4:47. The front desk coordinator — who has been on since 7:30, who has handled sixteen phone calls and checked in eleven patients and made three reactivation calls and navigated one difficult insurance conversation — gives this checkout the same quality of attention she gave the first interaction of the day.

"It was so great to see you today — Dr. [Name] was really pleased with how things looked. You're doing a wonderful job. We've got you on the schedule for October — we'll look forward to seeing you then. Take good care of yourself."

The patient smiles. Says she always enjoys coming in — that it never feels like going to the dentist. She means this as a compliment of the highest order.

She leaves.

The door closes.

After the Day

The team takes seven minutes at the end of the day — not a formal meeting, just a brief collective exhale and reflection.

The office manager asks: *"What went well today?"*

The hygienist mentions Sarah — the anxious patient who scheduled her next appointment before she left. The scheduling coordinator mentions Michael's reactivation call and the wife referral. The front desk coordinator mentions the insurance conversation that could have gone badly and did not.

Three wins. Named specifically. Celebrated briefly but genuinely.

The office manager asks: *"What do we want to do better tomorrow?"*

The conversation is brief and honest. One team member mentions a moment in a financial conversation that felt slightly awkward — a treatment estimate she fumbled slightly before finding her footing. The team offers language suggestions. Not criticism. Support.

Seven minutes. The team disperses.

Nobody leaves that practice feeling like they spent the day on a sales floor. Nobody leaves feeling like a performance metric. They leave feeling like people who spent their day doing something that mattered — who communicated with genuine care, who handled difficulty with grace, who built something real and lasting with every patient they served.

That feeling — experienced daily, over months and years — is what creates the staff retention that most practices can only dream of. The hygienist who has been there nine years. The front desk coordinator who turned down a better-paying offer two years ago because she did not want to leave. The scheduling coordinator who recommends the practice to her friends not as a place that is hiring but as a place worth belonging to.

Culture is not a program. It is not a set of scripts or a training system or a management philosophy.

It is a feeling. Built one conversation at a time. Sustained by leadership that models it daily. Reinforced by systems that keep it alive when the pressure builds.

And experienced — fully, genuinely, unmistakably — by every patient who walks through the door of a practice that has done the work.

What the Numbers Say

In a practice that has been operating with A.L.I.G.N.™ principles for twelve to eighteen months the metrics tell a specific and consistent story.

New patient phone conversion rates climb — from the industry average of 55 to 65 percent toward the 75 to 85 percent range that intentional phone communication produces. In a practice receiving twenty new patient inquiries per week that improvement represents three to five additional new patients per week. Fifty to one hundred additional new patients per year. At a conservative lifetime value of $3,000 per patient that is $150,000 to $300,000 in lifetime production — from phone language alone.

Case acceptance rates improve — moving from the national average of around 60 percent toward 75 to 85 percent in practices with strong treatment presentation language and a culture of patient-centered clinical communication. The financial impact of a fifteen-percentage-point improvement in case acceptance — across a practice producing $1.5 million annually — is measurable in hundreds of thousands of dollars of additional production from treatment that was already diagnosed, already appropriate, already waiting for the right conversation to move it forward.

Cancellation and no-show rates drop — sometimes dramatically — in practices that shift their confirmation language from questioning attendance to assuming it. A practice that reduces its no-show rate from twelve percent to six percent recovers dozens of appointment hours annually — production that was already on the schedule and simply needed the right language to stay there.

Reactivation success rates climb — from the single digits that most practices experience with guilt-based outreach toward twenty-five, thirty, thirty-five percent in practices whose reactivation language leads with genuine care.

Staff tenure increases. Review quality improves — not just in star rating but in the emotional language patients use, which shifts from clinical descriptions of technical quality toward personal descriptions of feeling cared for, seen, and genuinely valued.

These numbers are not hypothetical. They are the documented, consistent, observed outcomes of practices that have committed to the A.L.I.G.N.™ framework and implemented it with the consistency and leadership investment the system requires.

They are available to every practice.

Not as a guarantee. Not as an overnight transformation. But as the reliable, compounding, sustainable outcome of doing the right things — the communication things — consistently, intentionally, and with the genuine belief that the words matter.

Because the words matter.

John Maxwell has said it in a hundred different ways across a career spent studying what makes people and organizations grow. But perhaps never more simply or more powerfully than this:

"The most important single ingredient in the formula of success is knowing how to get along with people."

The practice that A.L.I.G.N.s has an attitude — a genuine, lived, daily-practiced, leadership-modeled attitude — of care. Of connection. Of the quiet but unwavering belief that every person who calls or walks through the door deserves to be treated as exactly that.

A person.

Not a production unit. Not a case acceptance statistic. Not an insurance verification. Not a reactivation opportunity.

A person.

With fears and financial realities and busy lives and the completely understandable human tendency to put off the things that feel uncomfortable until the moment when putting them off is no longer possible.

A person who called — or walked in — because somewhere in them they trust that this practice is worth trusting.

The practice that A.L.I.G.N.s earns that trust.

Every day.

One conversation at a time.

Chapter Takeaway

The practice that A.L.I.G.N.™s is not a perfect practice — it is a practice whose culture makes imperfection navigable. It is a practice where the morning huddle sets an intention rather than a logistical agenda, where new patients are welcomed rather than processed, where difficult conversations are handled with grace rather than defensiveness, and where team members end their days feeling that what they did mattered. The metrics of a fully aligned practice reflect not just better numbers but a better daily experience for every person inside the building — the team, the patients, and the leader who built something worth being proud of. The practice that A.L.I.G.N.™s did not get there through a single training event or a single coaching engagement. It got there through the consistent, daily, intentional application of five pillars that work together because they were built together. Awareness makes the gaps visible. Language fills them with trust. Identity makes the language genuine. Goals make the improvement measurable. Navigation makes it all permanent. That is what a fully aligned practice looks like. And it is available to every practice that decides to build it.

What This Means for Your Practice

I want to describe something for you. Not a hypothetical. Not a best-case scenario. Something I have watched happen in practice after practice when the A.L.I.G.N.™ work takes root.

The front desk coordinator who dreaded the fee question six months ago now handles it with the calm confidence of someone who has answered it a hundred times with the right words. She does not think about the language anymore. It is simply how she talks about fees — because it has become who she is professionally.

The scheduling coordinator who used to end confirmation calls with if you need to reschedule just give us a call now ends them with a genuine expression of anticipation. The cancellation rate in her call block dropped by six points in three months. She knows exactly why.

The dentist who used to walk past the front desk without acknowledging what was happening there now stops occasionally — specifically, genuinely — to say that call sounded great or I heard how you handled that patient and I want you to know that matters.

None of those people were transformed by a training program. They were developed by a system.

Here's What I Want You to Remember

The practice described above is not exceptional. It is available.

It is available to every practice whose leader decides — specifically, seriously, with the intention to sustain the decision through the systems this book describes — that the words their team chooses every day matter as much as the dentistry happening behind the operatory doors.

That decision is the beginning of everything.

And everything begins with the very next conversation your team has.

Chapter 16
Your 90-Day A.L.I.G.N.™ Implementation Plan

How to Go from Reading This Book to Living It

"The beginning is the most important part of the work." — John Maxwell

You have read fifteen chapters. You have followed the argument from its beginning — the words are costing you — through its middle — here is the system that changes that — and into its vision — here is what your practice looks like when the system works.

And if you are like most people who reach this point in a business book something is happening in your mind right now that is worth naming honestly.

You are inspired. You are motivated. You can see the practice this book describes and you want it — genuinely, specifically, with the clarity that comes from having read something that put language around things you have felt for years without being able to articulate them.

And somewhere underneath the inspiration — quiet but persistent — is the question that has undermined more good business books than any publisher would like to acknowledge:

"But where do I actually start?"

It is the right question. It is, in fact, the most important question a reader can ask at this point in the process — because the gap between inspiration and implementation is where the majority of practice improvement initiatives go to die. Not from lack of motivation. From lack of a specific, sequential, manageable plan that turns the big ideas into Monday morning actions.

This chapter is that plan.

Not a vague framework. Not a collection of principles to consider. A specific, week-by-week, action-oriented implementation guide that takes the five pillars of A.L.I.G.N.™ — Awareness, Language, Identity, Goals, and Navigation — and sequences them in the order that produces the fastest, most sustainable, most team-friendly transformation available.

Ninety days. That is the timeline. Not because practice transformation is complete in ninety days — it is not. But because ninety days of focused, consistent, daily action is enough time to establish the habits, systems, and cultural shifts that make everything that follows easier, more natural, and genuinely self-sustaining.

By day ninety your practice will not be perfect. It will be different. Measurably, observably, and — if you have done the work honestly — undeniably different in the ways that matter most.

That is the promise of this plan.

Let us begin.

"Success is not final, failure is not fatal: it is the courage to continue that counts." — John Maxwell

MONTH ONE — AWARENESS & LANGUAGE

Weeks 1 through 4

The governing principle of Month One:

See clearly. Then speak differently.

Month One is about two things — and only two things. Understanding exactly where the practice currently stands communicatively. And beginning to shift the specific language patterns that are creating the most friction and costing the most opportunity.

No system overhauls. No comprehensive team retraining. No leadership retreats or mission statement rewrites. Just honest observation and immediate, targeted language improvement — starting with the highest-impact conversations and working outward from there.

John Maxwell writes:

"To know thyself is the beginning of wisdom."

Month One gives the practice its sight.

Week 1 — The Awareness Audit

The objective: Understand specifically where the practice's communication is working and where it is not — before changing anything.

Day 1 through Day 3 — Listen.

The practice owner or office manager spends the first three days of the implementation in observation mode. Not correcting. Not coaching. Simply listening — with fresh ears and genuine curiosity — to the practice's actual communication as it happens.

Listen to the phone calls. How are new patient inquiries being handled? What language patterns are most common? Where does momentum shift in the conversation — and in which direction?

Listen to the confirmation calls. What phrase does the team use most often? Does it reinforce commitment or create an exit?

Listen to the checkout conversations. Are they warm and specific or transactional and brief?

Listen to the morning huddle — if one is happening. What is the emotional temperature? Is it logistical or intentional?

Write down what you hear. Not to build a case. To build a picture.

Day 4 — The Team Conversation.

Gather the team — not as a performance review but as a genuine collaborative exploration. Tell them honestly what you are doing and why.

"I've been paying close attention to how we communicate with our patients this week — not because anything is wrong, but because I want to understand where we are so we can figure out together where we want to be. I want to share what I noticed and hear what you've been experiencing."

Ask the team the language audit question introduced in Chapter 6: what are the three phrases you use most often in difficult patient interactions? Write them down together. Read them aloud together. Let the contrast do its work.

This conversation — conducted without blame and with genuine collaborative curiosity — is the single most important thirty minutes of the entire ninety-day process. It establishes the tone of everything that follows: that this practice is growing together, not being corrected from above.

Day 5 — The Numbers.

Pull the five communication metrics introduced in Chapter 8:

New patient phone conversion rate. Case acceptance rate. Cancellation and no-show rate. Reactivation success rate. Patient retention rate.

Some of these numbers will require a little digging. Some practices will not have easy access to all of them immediately — and that is fine. Get what you can get. Write down what you find. These are your baseline numbers — the starting point against which every improvement over the next ninety days will be measured.

If you do not know your numbers yet do not let that stop you from moving forward. Start tracking from this point forward. Ninety days from now you will have data.

Week 1 Deliverable: A clear, honest picture of where the practice currently stands — in its communication patterns, its team language habits, and its key metrics. Not a judgment. A starting point.

Week 2 — Phone Language

The objective: Transform the new patient phone call experience.

The phone call was chosen as the Week 2 focus for a specific reason — it is the highest-impact, most immediately changeable, and most measurable communication touchpoint in the practice. Improvements here produce visible results within days. And visible results in the first two weeks of implementation are enormously important for maintaining team motivation through the months that follow.

Day 1 — The Phone Language Workshop.

Conduct a thirty-minute team session specifically focused on the new patient phone call. Not a lecture — a practice session.

Using the five elements of the perfect new patient call from Chapter 10 as the framework — the warm opening, the discovery question, the acknowledgment, the confidence, the invitation — have team members practice the call with each other. Out loud. With real feedback.

This feels uncomfortable at first. That discomfort is useful. It reveals exactly where the language is uncertain and where it needs more practice before it meets a real patient.

Run the practice session multiple times. Switch roles. Have the office manager play the patient. Have the dentist play the scheduling coordinator. The role reversal produces insights that no amount of instruction can generate.

Day 2 through Day 4 — Implementation and Observation.

The new language goes live on the phones. Not perfectly — it will not be perfect in week two, and that is entirely expected and acceptable. The goal is not perfection. It is the beginning of a new habit.

The office manager or a designated observer listens to several calls per day — not to critique in real time but to gather observations for the daily debrief.

Day 5 — The Daily Debrief Begins.

This is a practice that starts in Week 2 and continues for the entire ninety days and beyond:

A five-minute end-of-day team check-in. One win — a communication moment that went well today. One learning — something that did not go as intended and what the team will try differently tomorrow.

Five minutes. Every day. The compound interest of daily reflection applied to communication improvement.

Week 2 Deliverable: A team that is actively practicing new phone language and beginning to build the daily debrief habit that will sustain improvement throughout the ninety days.

Week 3 — Confirmation and Scheduling Language

The objective: Close the exit ramps in scheduling and confirmation communication.

Having addressed the new patient call in Week 2 the focus now shifts to the language patterns that are giving scheduled patients permission to cancel.

Day 1 — The Confirmation Call Reset.

Review the confirmation call language currently in use. Identify the specific phrases — particularly any version of *"if you need to reschedule"* or *"are you still coming"* — that are planting cancellation seeds.

Replace them — as a team, collaboratively — with the assumptive confirmation language from Chapter 11. Practice it together until it feels natural. Record a sample voicemail with the new language. Listen to it together.

"Hi [Name] — this is [Name] from [Practice]. We're looking forward to seeing you tomorrow at two o'clock. We'll have everything ready for you. See you then!"

Simple. Warm. Confident. Practice it until every team member who makes confirmation calls can deliver it with genuine warmth rather than mechanical recitation.

Day 2 through Day 4 — Scheduling Language Practice.

Focus the daily debrief this week on scheduling conversations specifically. What is the team noticing? Where is the language feeling natural? Where is it still effortful?

Effortful is good. Effortful means the new habit has not yet displaced the old one — and that is entirely expected at week three. The practice is what closes that gap.

Day 5 — Track the First Numbers.

Two weeks into implementation pull the cancellation and no-show numbers for the week and compare them to your baseline. In some practices the improvement is already visible in week two or three — which is enormously motivating for the team.

Whether or not the numbers have moved yet the act of tracking them — of paying deliberate attention to a metric that was previously invisible — changes how the team thinks about the language. Numbers make the abstract concrete.

Week 3 Deliverable: New confirmation and scheduling language in daily use. Cancellation tracking begun. The team beginning to see the connection between language choices and measurable outcomes.

Week 4 — Financial and Insurance Language

The objective: Transform the money conversation from the most dreaded interaction in the practice to one of its most trust-building.

Day 1 — The Financial Language Audit.

Using the principles from Chapter 12 review the specific financial language currently in use at checkout, in treatment presentation, and in insurance conversations. Identify the specific phrases — *"you owe," "insurance won't cover," "you're maxed out"* — that are creating friction.

Replace them with the partnership-oriented language of A.L.I.G.N.™. Write the new phrases down. Post them where the financial conversations happen. Make them visible during the transition period.

Day 2 through Day 3 — Practice the Large Treatment Presentation.

Role-play the moment the large treatment estimate lands. Practice the response to the patient whose face does something complicated when they see the number. Practice the response to *"I can't afford it right now."*

These are the highest-stakes financial moments in the practice — and the ones most in need of specific, practiced language. Do not leave them to improvisation.

Day 4 — Insurance Language Integration.

Specifically practice the insurance advocacy language — the shift from passive messenger to active advocate. Role-play the most common insurance scenarios: out-of-network, frequency limitations, annual maximum, pre-estimates.

Practice until the new language feels as natural as the old language did — which it will not in week four, but which it will in month two.

Day 5 — Month One Review.

At the end of Week 4 conduct a slightly longer version of the daily debrief — fifteen minutes rather than five. Review the month:

What language has changed? What are team members noticing in their patient interactions? What metrics have moved? What feels natural now that felt effortful in Week 1?

Celebrate what has changed. Specifically and genuinely. Name the wins. Name the people who created them.

Set the intention for Month Two.

Month One Deliverable: A practice that has seen itself clearly, begun shifting its highest-impact language patterns, and established the daily debrief habit that sustains growth. A team that is communicating differently — not perfectly, but intentionally — and that is beginning to see the connection between their words and their outcomes.

MONTH TWO — IDENTITY & GOALS

Weeks 5 through 8

The governing principle of Month Two:

Know who you are. Then measure what matters.

Month Two deepens the work of Month One by addressing the two dimensions of practice development that most surface-level communication training never reaches — the identity of the practice and the goals that give its communication work direction, accountability, and momentum.

Week 5 — Leadership Identity Work

The objective: The practice owner examines — honestly and without defensiveness — the communication model they are setting for the team.

This is the most personal week of the ninety days. It asks the leader to do something that is rarely comfortable: to evaluate their own communication with the same honest curiosity they applied to the team's communication in Week 1.

Day 1 through Day 2 — The Leadership Self-Audit.

Using the questions from Chapter 7 the practice owner conducts a personal leadership communication review:

How do I respond when a team member makes a mistake? What language do I use? Does it open the door to growth or close it with shame?

What does my morning huddle communication model for the team? Am I present? Am I intentional? Am I communicating that the day's work is meaningful?

How do I talk about the practice — to team members, to patients, in the hallway, in the brief moments between appointments? Do my words reflect the identity I want the practice to have?

Write down the honest answers. Not to produce self-criticism. To produce self-knowledge. Because the leader who sees their own communication patterns clearly has the power to change them. The leader who cannot see them does not.

Day 3 through Day 5 — The Leadership Language Shift.

Identify the one specific leadership communication pattern — just one — that most needs to change. The most common candidates:

The way mistakes are addressed. The way the morning huddle is opened. The way challenging schedule days are discussed with the team. The way team member performance is referenced in group settings.

Choose one. Practice the shift — specifically, deliberately, in real interactions — for the rest of the week.

One change. Practiced consistently. Noticed by the team — often before the leader realizes they have noticed.

Week 5 Deliverable: A practice owner who has examined their own communication honestly and identified one specific leadership language shift to implement and sustain.

Week 6 — Practice Identity Articulation

The objective: Define — as a team — what this practice stands for communicatively.

Day 1 — The Identity Workshop.

Gather the team for a forty-five minute session built around three questions:

"How do we want patients to describe us when they leave — not clinically, but emotionally? What feeling do we want them to carry with them?"

"What do we do — consistently, in our best moments — that creates that feeling?"

"What is one thing we do — in our less best moments — that works against that feeling?"

Let the team answer. Write every answer down. Do not edit in the room.

After the session identify the common threads — the words and ideas that appeared in multiple answers. Those threads are the practice's genuine identity — not invented by a consultant, not imported from a mission statement template, but discovered in the actual values and aspirations of the people who work there every day.

Day 2 — The Identity Standard.

Distill the common threads into a single, clear, behavioral identity statement — specific enough to guide action, meaningful enough to inspire it.

Not *"we provide exceptional patient care."* That is every practice.

Something like: *"In this practice we treat every person who contacts us as if they are the most important call, the most important arrival, and the most important patient of the day — because to them, they are."*

Or: *"We are the practice where patients feel like people — not like patients."*

Write it down. Share it with the team. Put it somewhere visible — not as decoration but as a daily reminder of the standard everyone in the practice agreed to uphold.

Days 3 through 5 — The Onboarding Document.

Using the identity standard as its foundation draft the practice's communication culture document — the living description of how this practice communicates that will be given to every new team member from this point forward.

It does not need to be lengthy. One to two pages of clear, specific, values-based communication guidance. What we say. What we do not say. How we handle the difficult moments. What we are working toward together.

Week 6 Deliverable: A practice identity standard — owned by the team, not imposed on them — and the beginning of a communication culture document that will guide onboarding and team alignment for years.

Week 7 — Setting Communication Goals

The objective: Establish the specific, measurable communication targets that will drive accountability and celebrate progress through the rest of the ninety days and beyond.

Day 1 — The Goal-Setting Session.

Using the five communication metrics from Chapter 8 as the framework set specific ninety-day targets for each:

New patient phone conversion rate — current baseline and target. Case acceptance rate — current baseline and target. Cancellation and no-show rate — current baseline and target. Reactivation success rate — current baseline and target. Patient retention rate — current baseline and target.

Be ambitious but honest. A ten-percentage-point improvement in case acceptance in ninety days is achievable with consistent language work. A thirty-point improvement in ninety days is probably not — and setting unrealistic targets creates the discouragement that undermines motivation far more effectively than slow progress does.

Day 2 — Connect Goals to Financial Impact.

For each goal calculate the financial impact of achieving it. Use the framework from Chapter 8 — make the numbers visible and specific.

The goal of improving new patient conversion from 60 to 72 percent means approximately two additional new patients per week. At $3,000 average lifetime value that is $6,000 in lifetime production per week — $300,000 per year — from one metric.

Write these numbers down. Share them with the team. Not as pressure. As possibility.

Days 3 through 5 — The Tracking System.

Set up whatever simple tracking mechanism the practice will use to monitor the five metrics going forward. This does not need to be sophisticated. A shared spreadsheet. A section of the team communication board. A brief weekly report.

What matters is not the system's elegance but its consistency — the numbers need to be reviewed weekly to remain motivating. Numbers reviewed monthly lose their immediacy. Numbers reviewed weekly stay alive.

Week 7 Deliverable: Five specific communication goals with measurable targets. The financial impact of each goal calculated and visible. A simple, consistent tracking system in place.

Week 8 — The First Monthly Communication Review

The objective: Conduct the first formal monthly review of the practice's communication progress — and establish the monthly review as a permanent practice rhythm.

Following the structure from Chapter 8:

Open with celebration. What improved in Month One and the first weeks of Month Two? Where did the language work produce visible results?

Who had a conversation that exemplified the practice identity standard? Name it specifically. Name the person who created it.

Continue with honest assessment. Where are the metrics still below target? What patterns are still showing up that need continued work? What is the team finding most challenging?

Close with focus. Of all the areas where improvement is still needed what is the one thing the practice will focus on most intentionally in Month Three?

One thing.

The monthly communication review done right is one of the most motivating team experiences available to a dental practice — because it makes visible the progress that the daily work is producing. Team members who see their effort translated into specific, named improvements bring more of that effort to the next month's work.

Month Two Deliverable: A practice with a clear identity standard, specific measurable goals, a tracking system, and the monthly review habit that will sustain growth indefinitely. A leadership team whose communication is being deliberately aligned with the culture they want to create.

MONTH THREE — NAVIGATION

Weeks 9 through 12

The governing principle of Month Three:

Build it to last.

The first two months produced awareness, language improvement, identity clarity, and goal-setting. Month Three builds the systems that make all of it permanent — that ensure the culture the practice has begun to build survives time, turnover, and the inevitable pressures of growth.

Week 9 — The Onboarding System

The objective: Ensure that every future team member enters the practice's communication culture from day one rather than absorbing its habits through unguided observation.

Day 1 through Day 3 — Build the Onboarding Protocol.

Using the three-component framework from Chapter 9 build the practice's specific onboarding communication protocol:

The communication culture document — finalize the draft begun in Week 6. Review it. Refine it. Make it specific, readable, and genuinely reflective of who the practice has become.

The structured observation schedule — map out the specific observation experiences a new team member will have in their first week. Which phone calls will they shadow? Which patient interactions will they observe alongside an experienced team member? Who is responsible for debriefing those observations?

The early feedback structure — decide when the first communication check-in will happen for new team members, who will conduct it, and what questions it will ask.

Day 4 through Day 5 — Test It.

Have a current team member — ideally someone who went through the old onboarding experience — review the new protocol and give feedback. Would this have helped them? What is missing? What is unclear?

Revise based on their input. The team member whose perspective shapes the onboarding protocol is far more invested in its success than one who simply received it.

Week 9 Deliverable: A complete, tested, ready-to-use onboarding communication protocol that will transmit the practice's culture to every new team member from this point forward.

Week 10 — The Huddle System

The objective: Transform the morning huddle from a scheduling review into the daily cultural anchor it was always capable of being.

Day 1 — The Huddle Redesign.

Using the five-element structure from Chapter 9 redesign the morning huddle:

Schedule review with a communication lens. Language focus — one phrase, one principle, two minutes of practice. Win sharing. Challenge surfacing. Intention setting.

Write out the new structure. Practice it with the office manager or huddle leader. Time it — it should take ten to fifteen minutes maximum.

Days 2 through 5 — Implementation.

Run the new huddle format every morning for the rest of the week. It will feel slightly effortful at first — any new structure does. That effort is temporary. The habit, once established, becomes one of the most natural and valued rituals in the practice's day.

At the end of the week ask the team: *"How is the new huddle format feeling? What is working? What should we adjust?"*

Listen. Adjust. The huddle belongs to the team — the leader who treats it that way gets a team that protects it.

Week 10 Deliverable: A redesigned morning huddle running daily in its new format. A team that is beginning to feel the difference between a logistical morning meeting and an intentional communication preparation session.

Week 11 — The Performance Conversation System

The objective: Replace the annual review as the primary performance communication vehicle with the ongoing, growth-oriented monthly check-in system.

Day 1 — The System Design.

Using the four-question framework from Chapter 9 design the practice's monthly communication check-in structure:

What is working? What is one thing to focus on? What support do they need? How will we know it is improving?

Write out the questions. Decide who conducts the check-ins — practice owner, office manager, or a combination. Decide the frequency — monthly is the A.L.I.G.N.™ recommendation. Schedule the first round of check-ins for the final week of Month Three.

Day 2 — The Language of Coaching.

Before the check-ins begin invest one session in the language of coaching conversation — specifically, the language the practice owner and office manager will use in the check-ins themselves.

Because the check-in is itself a communication moment — and the quality of the leader's communication in that moment determines whether the team member experiences it as growth-oriented or evaluative.

Practice the opening. Practice the transition from *"what is working"* to *"what is one thing to focus on"* in a way that feels supportive rather than corrective. Practice the close — the specific, genuine acknowledgment of the team member's value and contribution.

Days 3 through 5 — Conduct the First Check-ins.

Begin the first round of monthly communication check-ins. Keep them to twenty minutes. Keep them focused. Keep them genuinely collaborative.

The first round will feel slightly formal — the structure is new and structure feels formal before it feels natural. That is fine. By the third month the check-ins will feel like conversations rather than meetings. By the sixth month team members will look forward to them.

Week 11 Deliverable: A monthly performance check-in system in place and running. Every team member has had or is scheduled for their first communication growth conversation.

Week 12 — Integration and the 90-Day Review

The objective: Consolidate everything built in ninety days. Celebrate what has been created. Set the direction for what comes next.

Day 1 through Day 3 — The Evolution System Setup.

Using the three components from Chapter 9 establish the practice's Evolution System:

Schedule the first quarterly communication audit — three months from now. Put it on the calendar. Assign responsibility. Decide what it will examine.

Plan the annual culture assessment — twelve months from now. Decide what questions it will ask. Decide who will lead it.

Create the new challenge protocol — the simple, agreed-upon process for developing communication responses when something significant changes in the practice. Who is responsible? What is the timeline? How does the response get developed and implemented?

The Evolution System does not need to be elaborate. It needs to be scheduled — because things that are not scheduled do not happen.

Day 4 — The 90-Day Communication Review.

This is the extended version of the monthly communication review — a comprehensive look back at the ninety days and a clear-eyed setting of direction for what follows.

Start with the metrics. Pull all five communication metrics and compare them to the baselines established in Week 1. Where has the practice improved? By how much? What does that improvement mean in financial terms — be specific, be honest, celebrate what is real.

Review the identity. Does the practice feel different communicatively than it did ninety days ago? Ask the team. Ask specific questions — not *"are things better"* but *"what do you notice about how we communicate now compared to how we communicated in the beginning?"* The answers will be the most motivating data point of the entire ninety days.

Review the systems. Is the onboarding protocol ready for the next new hire? Is the huddle running consistently? Are the monthly check-ins happening? Is the tracking system being maintained?

Identify the gaps honestly. Where is the practice still below target? What is the one thing that needs the most focused attention in the next ninety days?

Day 5 — The Celebration and the Next Step.

The final day of the ninety-day implementation is a day for two things.

Celebration. Genuine, specific, named celebration of what the practice has built — the language that has changed, the systems that are in place, the metrics that have moved, the team that did the work. Not a party. A moment of honest acknowledgment that something real was created here — and that the people in this practice are the ones who created it.

And the next step. Because ninety days is a beginning — a strong, significant, momentum-building beginning — not an ending.

The practice that has completed this plan has established the foundation of an A.L.I.G.N.™ culture. It has the awareness to see itself clearly. The language to communicate with care and confidence. The identity to know what it stands for. The goals to measure what matters. The navigation systems to sustain and grow everything it has built.

What it does with that foundation — in the ninety days that follow, and the ninety after that, and the years of compounding growth and deepening culture that stretch beyond the horizon of any implementation plan — is the story the practice gets to write for itself.

John Maxwell — who has spent his career helping people understand that growth is not an event but a daily practice — closes this thought better than anyone:

"You will never change your life until you change something you do daily. The secret of your success is found in your daily routine."

The daily routine of an A.L.I.G.N.™ practice — the morning huddle, the intentional phone call, the warm greeting, the patient-centered treatment conversation, the confident financial discussion, the coaching check-in, the five-minute end-of-day reflection — is the secret.

Not the secret of a weekend retreat. Not the secret of a consulting engagement. The secret of a daily practice — built one conversation at a time, sustained one habit at a time, and compounding in ways that no production report can fully capture but that every patient who walks through the door feels the moment they arrive.

A Final Word Before You Begin

I want to say one more thing before you close this book and open your calendar to Week 1.

Do not wait for the perfect moment to start. There is no perfect moment. There is only Monday morning — and the decision to begin.

Do not wait until the team is ready. The team will become ready by doing the work — not by thinking about it or discussing it or planning for it indefinitely.

Do not wait until you have more time. You will not have more time. You have exactly the time you have — and the practices that transform are the ones that choose to use it differently, not the ones that wait for the schedule to clear.

The practice you have been reading about throughout this book — the one that communicates with genuine care, that retains its patients through authentic connection, that grows because it serves exceptionally well — is not a distant aspiration.

It is ninety days away.

It is one morning huddle away.

It is one phone call — handled differently, with more warmth and more intention than the one before it — away.

Begin.

John Maxwell — who I believe would recognize in A.L.I.G.N.™ the practical application of principles he has spent a lifetime teaching — says it with his characteristic clarity and conviction:

"It's not what we do once in a while that shapes our lives. It's what we do consistently."

Change the agenda. Change the conversations. Change the practice.

It starts today.

Your 90-Day A.L.I.G.N.™ Implementation Plan — At a Glance

Month One — Awareness & Language

- Week 1: The Awareness Audit — listen, observe, gather baseline metrics
- Week 2: Phone Language — transform the new patient call experience
- Week 3: Confirmation and Scheduling Language — close the exit ramps
- Week 4: Financial and Insurance Language — make money conversations trust-building

Month Two — Identity & Goals

- Week 5: Leadership Identity Work — examine and shift the model you set
- Week 6: Practice Identity Articulation — define who you are as a team
- Week 7: Setting Communication Goals — establish metrics and targets
- Week 8: First Monthly Communication Review — celebrate, assess, focus

Month Three — Navigation

- Week 9: The Onboarding System — transmit culture to every new team member
- Week 10: The Huddle System — make the morning huddle a cultural anchor
- Week 11: The Performance Conversation System — replace reviews with coaching
- Week 12: Integration and 90-Day Review — celebrate, measure, set direction

Chapter Takeaway

What This Means for Your Practice

The ninety-day A.L.I.G.N.™ implementation plan translates the five pillars of the system into a specific, week-by-week sequence of actions that produces measurable, sustainable practice transformation. Month One focuses on Awareness and Language — seeing the practice clearly and beginning to shift its highest-impact communication patterns. Month Two focuses on Identity and Goals — defining who the practice is and setting the specific communication targets that drive accountability. Month Three focuses on Navigation — building the onboarding, huddle, performance, and evolution systems that make everything else permanent. The plan is not the destination. It is the road. And the road begins with a single step — taken on Monday morning, in the next phone call, in the next huddle, in the next patient interaction — that is spoken just a little differently, with just a little more intention, than the one before it. That is where transformation begins. That is where it has always begun. In the next conversation.

We have arrived at the chapter that everything before it was building toward.

Not because the previous fifteen chapters were preparation for the real work. They were the real work. The awareness you developed. The language you examined. The identity questions you sat with honestly. The goals you set specifically. The navigation systems you began to understand.

All of it matters. All of it is essential. And all of it now needs one more thing to become genuinely transformative rather than genuinely interesting.

It needs to be implemented.

Not perfectly. Not all at once. Not with the anxiety of someone who feels the weight of sixteen chapters pressing down on the first Monday morning of the implementation.

Here's What I Want You to Remember

One week at a time. One focus at a time. One specific language change practiced consistently until it becomes automatic — and then the next one.

Start this week. Not next month when things settle down. Not after the next team meeting. This week.

Pick one thing from the 90-day plan — the phone audit, the Team Language Inventory, the conversation with the dentist about buy-in. Pick the one that feels most immediately possible and do it before Friday.

Because the practice that starts imperfectly this week will always outperform the practice that waits for the perfect moment that never quite arrives.

The next word your team speaks is the beginning. Make it the right one.

Conclusion

The Conversation That Changes Everything

"Leaders must be close enough to relate to others, but far enough ahead to motivate them." — John Maxwell

There is a conversation that changed everything.

Not the one you are thinking of. Not a dramatic conversation — not a confrontation or a revelation or a moment of sudden clarity delivered in the kind of cinematic circumstances that make for good stories but rarely reflect how real change actually arrives.

This conversation was quiet. Ordinary by every external measure. It happened in a dental office — at the front desk, on a Tuesday morning, on a phone call that lasted **four minutes and seventeen seconds**.

A woman called. She had been putting off the call for eight months. Not because she did not care about her teeth. Because she was afraid — of the cost, of the judgment, of the gap between her last visit and this one, of the particular vulnerability of sitting in a dental chair and being examined by someone who would see every consequence of the years of avoidance.

She almost did not call.

But she did.

And the person who answered the phone said something that surprised her. Not with extraordinary words — there was no speech, no performance, no carefully constructed sales approach. Just warmth. Just genuine interest. Just the simple, powerful, entirely uncommon experience of being made to feel welcome before she had even explained why she was calling.

She scheduled an appointment.

She came in.

She sat in the chair — nervous, slightly braced for judgment — and received instead exactly what the phone call had promised. Care. Attention. The specific, personal, unhurried experience of being treated as someone who mattered.

She became a patient.

She stayed for eleven years. She referred her husband, her children, her sister, two colleagues, and a neighbor she barely knew who mentioned in passing that she was looking for a dentist. She left reviews that other patients mentioned when they called. She recommended the practice with the particular enthusiasm of someone who was not just satisfied but genuinely grateful — who felt that finding this practice was a small but real stroke of luck in the ordinary course of her life.

All of that.

From one conversation.

From **four minutes and seventeen seconds** of intentional, warm, genuine human communication.

From the decision — made by one person, at one front desk, on one Tuesday morning — to answer the phone as if the person on the other end of it was someone worth showing up fully for.

"The greatest gift you can give someone is the gift of your time and attention." — John Maxwell

This book has been about words. About the specific, practical, immediately applicable language that transforms dental practice communication from a source of friction, lost patients, and missed production into the most powerful growth engine available to any practice.

But underneath the words — underneath every language example, every communication principle, every A.L.I.G.N.™ framework and implementation strategy — there is something that is not about words at all.

It is about what the words represent.

Because the words in this book are not techniques. They are not sales approaches or closing strategies or persuasion tools. They are the external expression of an internal commitment — the commitment to treat every human being who contacts your practice as exactly that.

A human being.

With fears worth acknowledging. With financial realities worth respecting. With a story worth being curious about. With the completely reasonable expectation that the people responsible for their oral health will show up for them — not just clinically, not just technically, but humanly.

That commitment is not a communication strategy.

It is a value.

And the A.L.I.G.N.™ system — in all its practical, specific, metric-driven, language-focused, system-building detail — is simply the mechanism for making that value visible. For translating the genuine care that most dental professionals already feel into the specific words, habits, and cultural practices that communicate it reliably to every patient, in every interaction, on every Tuesday morning when the phone rings and someone on the other end of the line is working up the courage to ask for help.

What This Book Asked of You

If you read these sixteen chapters honestly — if you applied the awareness exercises and recognized your practice's blind spots, if you read the language examples and winced at the familiar phrases, if you reached the vision chapter and felt the specific ache of wanting what was described there — then this book asked something of you.

It asked you to look.

To look at the gap between the practice you have and the practice you are capable of being. To look at the words your team uses and ask — honestly and without defensiveness — whether those words are serving your patients and your practice or quietly working against both. To look at your own leadership communication and consider whether the culture you model is the culture you want your patients to experience.

Looking is not comfortable. Looking at gaps rarely is.

But looking is the beginning of everything. It is the Awareness at the foundation of A.L.I.G.N.™ — the clear sight without which no change is possible and with which no change is impossible.

You looked.

That matters.

Now the book asks one more thing.

What Comes Next

Act!

Not comprehensively. Not perfectly. Not with the kind of total organizational overhaul that sounds impressive in a planning meeting and collapses under the weight of a busy Tuesday morning.

Act in the small, specific, immediately available ways that this book described throughout its ninety-day plan.

Answer the next phone call as if the person on the other end of it is someone worth showing up fully for.

Open tomorrow's morning huddle with a question about how you want your patients to feel rather than a review of the production schedule.

Make one reactivation call today that leads with *"we've been thinking about you"* instead of *"you're overdue."*

Present the next treatment recommendation in the language of preservation rather than loss.

Handle the next financial conversation with the quiet confidence of a practice that knows its care is worth what it charges.

These are not dramatic actions. They do not require a budget or a consultant or a weekend retreat or an organizational transformation initiative.

They require only the decision — made once, and then made again tomorrow, and again the day after — to communicate with more intention than yesterday.

That decision — compounded daily, sustained by the systems this book described, modeled by the leadership this book challenged, and measured by the metrics this book introduced — is the entire A.L.I.G.N.™ system in its most fundamental form.

It is the decision to be better — not someday, not when the conditions are perfect — but now. In the next conversation. With the next patient. In the next moment when a word could either build a bridge or a wall and you choose, deliberately and intentionally, to build the bridge.

John Maxwell's work found me nine years ago — and it has not left me since.

In 38 years of working inside dental practices I have encountered a great deal of leadership theory and communication methodology. None of it has shaped the way I think, coach, and lead quite like John Maxwell's body of work. His understanding of leadership, communication, and human development is the most practically useful framework I have ever studied — and the most directly applicable to the real challenges dental practices face every single day.

Nine years ago I became a certified John Maxwell Team Member. That decision deepened the philosophy behind A.L.I.G.N.™ and gave me the privilege of bringing his methodology directly into the practices I serve.

You will hear his voice throughout these pages. Not as decoration. As foundation.

He says it simply and finally:

"Today is the most important day of your life."

Not yesterday — which cannot be changed. Not tomorrow — which cannot be guaranteed. Today. This conversation. This phone call. This huddle. This treatment presentation. This moment when a patient looks to your team for something more than clinical competence — for the feeling of being genuinely cared for by people who chose this work because they wanted to make a difference in the lives of the people they serve.

Today is the most important day.

Make today's conversations worthy of it.

The Ripple

I want to close with one final thought — one that extends beyond the practice, beyond the production metrics, beyond even the extraordinary patient relationships that A.L.I.G.N.™ communication builds.

Every conversation your practice has — every phone call handled with warmth, every treatment presented with genuine care, every financial discussion conducted with confidence and partnership, every team member developed through coaching rather than criticism — creates a ripple.

The new patient who called nervously and was received warmly goes home that evening and tells her husband about the practice. He makes an appointment. Their daughter eventually becomes a patient. The husband mentions the practice to a colleague who mentions it to his wife. The ripple moves outward — invisibly, unmeasurably, but with perfect reliability — from that one phone call, that one moment of genuine human connection.

Multiply that ripple by every conversation your practice has in a year. By every patient who felt genuinely cared for and told someone. By every team member who loved their work enough to recommend the practice to their own family. By every review that began with *"I actually look forward to going to the dentist"* and that the next anxious caller read before deciding to make the call they had been putting off for eight months.

The ripple is not abstract. It is the compounding return on every investment of intentional communication — paid out not in a single quarter but over the years and decades of a practice's life, in the form of patients who stay and patients who refer and team members who remain and a reputation that no marketing budget could manufacture.

It starts with a conversation.

It starts with the decision to have that conversation differently than you have been having it.

It starts with the next call.

"Better conversations. Better connections. Bigger impact."

That is not just a tagline.

It is a promise.

A promise this book was written to help you keep — with every patient, every team member, every day.

Go keep it

About the Author

Tammy Duncan is a leadership and practice growth professional dedicated to transforming dental teams — building stronger communication, healthier culture, and the kind of sustainable operational systems that make practices genuinely great places to work and genuinely exceptional places to receive care.

Her journey to the coaching world is unlike most. Tammy has lived the operational and administrative side of dental practice from the inside — as a dental assistant working chairside, as an office manager running daily operations, and as a software trainer for one of the industry's top practice management software companies. That path gave her something most consultants and coaches simply do not have — the lived experience of the roles that determine whether a dental practice thrives or struggles every single day. She has worked chairside. She has run the front desk. She has trained teams on the systems that run the daily operations of some of the most successful practices in the country. She knows what dental teams face not from the outside looking in — but from the inside out.

Since co-founding Practice Management Systems® in 2006 alongside her husband and business partner David Duncan — Tammy has been building a dental coaching company grounded in the belief that the strongest practices are built through clarity, consistency, encouragement, and leadership that develops people, not just systems.

As creator of the A.L.I.G.N.™ Private Practice Growth Program, Tammy brings a practical, people-centered approach to leadership development inside private dental practices. Her passion for team communication, patient connection, accountability, and organizational growth shaped the A.L.I.G.N.™ framework into a real-world system designed to support both practice performance and team well-being — simultaneously and sustainably.

A certified John Maxwell Team Member, Tammy's approach to leadership development is grounded in one of the most respected methodologies in the world — and applied specifically to the daily realities of dental practice life. She believes that the strongest practices are not built on systems alone. They are built on leaders who communicate with clarity, develop their people with intentionality, and create cultures where both teams and patients feel genuinely valued.

Her work focuses on elevating dental teams — improving confidence, communication, and daily operational effectiveness through the kind of simple but powerful conversations that create lasting transformation, not temporary motivation.

Dental assistant. Office manager. Software trainer. Dental coach. And now — author.

Four Minutes and Seventeen Seconds is Tammy's first book — and the most complete expression of everything she has learned across a career spent inside the dental practice, at every level, in every role, always asking the same question:

What if the words we choose could change everything?

— Tammy Duncan Practice Management Systems 2026

Acknowledgments

Every book begins long before the first word is written. This one began in the hallways of dental practices, in morning huddles, in difficult conversations, and in the quiet moments between appointments where something true about how people communicate — and how they fail to — revealed itself one observation at a time. None of what fills these pages would exist without the people who filled my life while I was learning it.

To my husband and business partner **David Duncan** — you are the steadiest person I know. You believed in this book before I did, in this business before the world did, and in me through every season of both. None of this exists without you. None of it would be worth doing without you beside me.

To my daughter **Amanda** — your strength, your grace, and the beautiful family you have built fill me with more pride than I know how to put into words. And to **Riley** and **Brody** — you remind me every single day why the work of building something lasting matters.

To my daughter **Alyssa** — your energy and love for life are contagious in the best possible way. And to **Sadie**, **Allie**, and **Tatum** — three reasons to smile without even trying. Being your grandmother is one of the greatest privileges of my life.

To **John Maxwell** and his extraordinary team of business and speaking coaches — your investment in developing leaders has shaped not just this book but the way I see every room I walk into. Being a certified member of the John Maxwell Team is one of the honors I carry most seriously. Your fingerprints are on every page of this work.

And finally — to every dental team member who has ever answered the phone on a busy Tuesday morning, handled a difficult financial conversation with grace, or found the right words in a moment when the wrong ones would have been so much easier —

This book is for you.

You are the reason four minutes and seventeen seconds can change everything.

— Tammy Duncan Practice Management Systems® 2026

How to Work with Us

Every dental practice reaches a moment when someone hears their own words from the outside for the first time.

A confirmation call. A financial conversation through the patient's eyes.

Once you see it, you can't unsee it.

That's what Practice Management Systems® creates—for practices ready to stop losing patients and production to the words no one thought to examine.

Start Here — Free Practice Communication Assessment

Thirty to forty-five minutes. No obligation. No pitch. Just an honest conversation about where your practice stands communicatively — what is working, what is costing you, and what the highest-impact changes would be for your specific team and goals.

The A.L.I.G.N.™ In-Office Workshop — 4 Hour *Real Results. Starting Monday.*

Four hours. Your office. Your schedule. Your team experiences the recognition moment, receives the specific "Instead Of" language for the five highest-impact communication scenarios in your practice, practices it out loud with real feedback, and leaves with a clear 30-day action plan.

Not a motivational talk. Two hours of specific, immediately applicable communication development from someone with 38 years inside practices exactly like yours.

The A.L.I.G.N.™ Communication Transformation Event — Six Hours
The Full Transformation. In a Single Day.

For the practice ready to go all the way. Six hours at an off-site venue. All five pillars. Your team experiences the recognition moment, masters the Instead Of language for every high-stakes patient conversation, completes the Practice Identity Workshop, sets specific 90-day goals connected to real practice metrics, and walks out with their complete 90-Day Implementation Plan — with lunch included and Tammy working personally with every attendee throughout the day.

Every attendee leaves with the "Instead Of" Language Reference Card, the 90-Day Implementation workbook, their personal public commitment, and a signed copy of *Four Minutes and Seventeen Seconds*. Within 48 hours every attendee receives a personal follow-up email from Tammy sustaining the momentum into the following week.

Six hours that change how your practice sounds — to every patient, in every conversation, starting the very next morning.

The A.L.I.G.N.™ Private Practice Growth Program *The Complete Transformation*

For the practice ready to build something permanent. A fully customized coaching engagement through all five pillars — with the depth and daily systems that produce a communication culture sustaining itself long after the coaching ends.

Practices consistently see new patient conversion rates climb into the 75 to 85 percent range, case acceptance improve by fifteen to twenty percentage points, cancellation rates drop, and staff retention improve.

Bring Tammy to Your Stage

Keynote presentations and custom team training for dental associations, study clubs, and dental groups. Every audience leaves with something they can use Monday morning.

Not sure where to start? Begin with the free assessment or the two-hour workshop — then decide what comes next.

Practice Management Systems®
www.practice-sys.com
(503) 449-1618

Notes and Citations

Four Minutes and Seventeen Seconds: How One Conversation Changes Everything in a Dental Practice

By Tammy Duncan, Practice Management Systems®

A Note on John Maxwell

John Maxwell's words appear throughout this book because his thinking has shaped mine more than any other voice in my professional life. I am a certified John Maxwell Team Member and I encourage every reader to explore his complete body of work. All Maxwell quotes are used with deep personal gratitude and full attribution to their original sources. The breadth of his influence on the philosophy behind A.L.I.G.N.™ cannot be overstated.

A Note on Attribution

Several quotes used in this book — particularly those attributed to Abraham Lincoln, Theodore Roosevelt, Winston Churchill, Maya Angelou, and George Bernard Shaw — are widely circulated in leadership literature and are sometimes attributed to multiple sources. Where attribution is disputed or uncertain, the most commonly accepted source is cited and noted accordingly. Readers are encouraged to verify primary sources independently.

Citations by Chapter

The following citations are organized by chapter in order of appearance. Full bibliographic information for each source appears in the Master Bibliography beginning on the following page.

Introduction — The Most Expensive Sentence in Dentistry

Shaw, George Bernard (attributed).

"The single biggest problem in communication is the illusion that it has taken place."

Widely attributed to George Bernard Shaw and frequently cited by John Maxwell in leadership contexts. Original source unverified in Shaw's published works. See Maxwell, John C. Everyone Communicates, Few Connect. Nashville: Thomas Nelson, 2010.

Chapter 1 — The Words Are Costing You

Maxwell, John C.

"People may hear your words, but they feel your attitude."

Maxwell, John C. The Maxwell Daily Reader: 365 Days of Insight to Develop the Leader Within You and Influence Those Around You. Nashville: Thomas Nelson, 2007.

Shaw, George Bernard (attributed).

"The single biggest problem in communication is the illusion that it has taken place."

Widely attributed to George Bernard Shaw. Frequently cited by Maxwell, John C. in Everyone Communicates, Few Connect. Nashville: Thomas Nelson, 2010.

Maxwell, John C.

"Small disciplines repeated with consistency every day lead to great achievements gained slowly over time."

Maxwell, John C. The 15 Invaluable Laws of Growth: Live Them and Reach Your Potential. Nashville: Center Street, 2012.

Chapter 2 — The Team Is Not the Problem. The Training Is.

Maxwell, John C.

"A leader's job is not to do the work for others, it's to help others figure out how to do it themselves, to get things done, and to succeed beyond what they thought possible."

Maxwell, John C. The 360 Degree Leader: Developing Your Influence from Anywhere in the Organization. Nashville: Thomas Nelson, 2005.

Maxwell, John C.

"The growth and development of people is the highest calling of leadership."

Maxwell, John C. Developing the Leader Within You. Nashville: Thomas Nelson, 1993.

Maxwell, John C.

"A leader who produces other leaders multiplies their influences."

Maxwell, John C. The 21 Irrefutable Laws of Leadership: Follow Them and People Will Follow You. Nashville: Thomas Nelson, 1998.

Chapter 3 — Why Great Training Deserves a Great System

Maxwell, John C.

"People buy into the leader before they buy into the vision."

Maxwell, John C. The 21 Irrefutable Laws of Leadership: Follow Them and People Will Follow You. Nashville: Thomas Nelson, 1998.

Maxwell, John C.

"Leadership is not about the next election, it's about the next generation."

Maxwell, John C. Leadership Gold: Lessons I've Learned from a Lifetime of Leading. Nashville: Thomas Nelson, 2008.

Maxwell, John C.

"You'll never change your life until you change something you do daily. The secret of your success is found in your daily routine."

Maxwell, John C. The 15 Invaluable Laws of Growth: Live Them and Reach Your Potential. Nashville: Center Street, 2012.

Chapter 4 — What Is A.L.I.G.N.™?

Maxwell, John C.

"A dream is just a dream. A goal is a dream with a plan and a deadline."

Maxwell, John C. Put Your Dream to the Test: 10 Questions to Help You See It and Seize It. Nashville: Thomas Nelson, 2009.

Aristotle (attributed).

"The whole is greater than the sum of its parts."

Paraphrase of Aristotle's concept in Metaphysica, c. 350 BCE. Public domain. Cited in Maxwell, John C. The 17 Indisputable Laws of Teamwork: Embrace Them and Empower Your Team. Nashville: Thomas Nelson, 2001.

Maxwell, John C.

"Awareness is the first step toward change. You cannot fix what you cannot see."

Maxwell, John C. Intentional Living: Choosing a Life That Matters. Nashville: Center Street, 2015.

Maxwell, John C.

"Everything rises and falls on leadership."

Maxwell, John C. The 21 Irrefutable Laws of Leadership: Follow Them and People Will Follow You. Nashville: Thomas Nelson, 1998.

Maxwell, John C.

"Dreams don't work unless you do."

Maxwell, John C. The Maxwell Daily Reader: 365 Days of Insight to Develop the Leader Within You and Influence Those Around You. Nashville: Thomas Nelson, 2007.

Chapter 5 — A is for Awareness

Maxwell, John C.

"The greatest mistake we make is living in constant fear that we will make one."

Maxwell, John C. Failing Forward: Turning Mistakes into Stepping Stones for Success. Nashville: Thomas Nelson, 2000.

Maxwell, John C.

"We cannot become what we need to be by remaining what we are."

Maxwell, John C. The 21 Irrefutable Laws of Leadership: Follow Them and People Will Follow You. Nashville: Thomas Nelson, 1998.

Maxwell, John C.

"One of the greatest gifts you can give people is the gift of your attention."

Maxwell, John C. Everyone Communicates, Few Connect: What the Most Effective People Do Differently. Nashville: Thomas Nelson, 2010.

Maxwell, John C.

"The more seriously you take your growth, the more seriously your team will take theirs."

Maxwell, John C. The 15 Invaluable Laws of Growth: Live Them and Reach Your Potential. Nashville: Center Street, 2012.

Maxwell, John C.

"A good leader is a person who takes a little more than his share of the blame and a little less than his share of the credit."

Maxwell, John C. The 21 Indispensable Qualities of a Leader: Becoming the Person Others Will Want to Follow. Nashville: Thomas Nelson, 1999.

Maxwell, John C.

"You don't have to be great to start, but you have to start to be great."

Maxwell, John C. The Maxwell Daily Reader: 365 Days of Insight to Develop the Leader Within You and Influence Those Around You. Nashville: Thomas Nelson, 2007.

Chapter 6 — L is for Language

Maxwell, John C.

"Words are free. It's how you use them that may cost you."

Maxwell, John C. Everyone Communicates, Few Connect: What the Most Effective People Do Differently. Nashville: Thomas Nelson, 2010.

Maxwell, John C. (attributed).

"The tongue has no bones, but is strong enough to break a heart. So be careful with your words."

Widely attributed in leadership literature. Cited in Maxwell, John C. Everyone Communicates, Few Connect. Nashville: Thomas Nelson, 2010. Original attribution disputed.

Maxwell, John C.

"The most important thing in communication is hearing what isn't said."

Maxwell, John C. Everyone Communicates, Few Connect: What the Most Effective People Do Differently. Nashville: Thomas Nelson, 2010.

Maxwell, John C.

"Communication is not just words. It is the tone, intent, and emotion behind the words."

Maxwell, John C. Everyone Communicates, Few Connect: What the Most Effective People Do Differently. Nashville: Thomas Nelson, 2010.

Maxwell, John C.

"A leader's words carry extra weight. Choose them accordingly."

Maxwell, John C. Leadership Gold: Lessons I've Learned from a Lifetime of Leading. Nashville: Thomas Nelson, 2008.

Chapter 7 — I is for Identity

Maxwell, John C.

"Everything rises and falls on leadership."

Maxwell, John C. The 21 Irrefutable Laws of Leadership: Follow Them and People Will Follow You. Nashville: Thomas Nelson, 1998.

Maxwell, John C.

"Leadership is influence — nothing more, nothing less."

Maxwell, John C. The 21 Irrefutable Laws of Leadership: Follow Them and People Will Follow You. Nashville: Thomas Nelson, 1998.

Maxwell, John C.

"Image is what people think we are. Integrity is what we really are."

Maxwell, John C. The 21 Indispensable Qualities of a Leader: Becoming the Person Others Will Want to Follow. Nashville: Thomas Nelson, 1999.

Maxwell, John C.

"The difference between a boss and a leader: a boss says 'Go!' — a leader says 'Let's go!'"

Maxwell, John C. Developing the Leader Within You. Nashville: Thomas Nelson, 1993.

Chapter 8 — G is for Goals

Maxwell, John C.

"A dream is just a dream. A goal is a dream with a plan and a deadline."

Maxwell, John C. Put Your Dream to the Test: 10 Questions to Help You See It and Seize It. Nashville: Thomas Nelson, 2009.

Robbins, Tony.

"Setting goals is the first step in turning the invisible into the visible."

Robbins, Anthony. Awaken the Giant Within: How to Take Immediate Control of Your Mental, Emotional, Physical and Financial Destiny. New York: Free Press, 1991. Cited frequently alongside John Maxwell in leadership development contexts.

Maxwell, John C.

"You cannot improve what you do not measure. And you cannot measure what you do not define."

Maxwell, John C. The 17 Indisputable Laws of Teamwork: Embrace Them and Empower Your Team. Nashville: Thomas Nelson, 2001.

Maxwell, John C.

"People don't care how much you know until they know how much you care."

Maxwell, John C. The 21 Irrefutable Laws of Leadership: Follow Them and People Will Follow You. Nashville: Thomas Nelson, 1998.

Maxwell, John C.

"Motivation gets you going but discipline keeps you growing."

Maxwell, John C. The 15 Invaluable Laws of Growth: Live Them and Reach Your Potential. Nashville: Center Street, 2012.

Maxwell, John C.

"Leaders become great not because of their power but because of their ability to empower others."

Maxwell, John C. The 21 Irrefutable Laws of Leadership: Follow Them and People Will Follow You. Nashville: Thomas Nelson, 1998.

Maxwell, John C.

"The secret of your success is determined by your daily agenda."

Maxwell, John C. Today Matters: 12 Daily Practices to Guarantee Tomorrow's Success. Nashville: Center Street, 2004.

Chapter 9 — N is for Navigation

Maxwell, John C.

"A leader who produces other leaders multiplies their influences."

Maxwell, John C. The 21 Irrefutable Laws of Leadership: Follow Them and People Will Follow You. Nashville: Thomas Nelson, 1998.

Maxwell, John C.

"The pessimist complains about the wind. The optimist expects it to change. The leader adjusts the sails."

Maxwell, John C. Leadership Gold: Lessons I've Learned from a Lifetime of Leading. Nashville: Thomas Nelson, 2008.

Maxwell, John C.

"Successful and unsuccessful people do not vary greatly in their abilities. They vary in their desires to reach their potential."

Maxwell, John C. The 21 Irrefutable Laws of Leadership: Follow Them and People Will Follow You. Nashville: Thomas Nelson, 1998.

Maxwell, John C.

"The greatest day in your life and mine is when we take total responsibility for our attitudes. That's the day we truly grow up."

Maxwell, John C. The Difference Maker: Making Your Attitude Your Greatest Asset. Nashville: Thomas Nelson, 2006.

Maxwell, John C.

"The ultimate leader is one who is willing to develop people to the point that they eventually surpass him or her in knowledge and ability."

Maxwell, John C. Developing the Leader Within You. Nashville: Thomas Nelson, 1993.

Chapter 10 — The New Patient Experience

Maxwell, John C.

"You never get a second chance to make a first impression — so make the first impression count."

Maxwell, John C. Everyone Communicates, Few Connect: What the Most Effective People Do Differently. Nashville: Thomas Nelson, 2010.

Maxwell, John C.

"Connecting is the ability to identify with people and relate to them in a way that increases your influence with them."

Maxwell, John C. Everyone Communicates, Few Connect: What the Most Effective People Do Differently. Nashville: Thomas Nelson, 2010.

Maxwell, John C.

"People don't care how much you know until they know how much you care."

Maxwell, John C. The 21 Irrefutable Laws of Leadership: Follow Them and People Will Follow You. Nashville: Thomas Nelson, 1998.

Chapter 11 — Scheduling and Appointment Control

Maxwell, John C. (attributed to Aristotle).

"We are what we repeatedly do. Excellence, then, is not an act, but a habit."

Paraphrase of Aristotle's Nicomachean Ethics, c. 350 BCE, as rendered by Will Durant in The Story of Philosophy (1926). Public domain. Widely cited by Maxwell, John C. in leadership development contexts.

Maxwell, John C.

"The difference between where we are and where we want to be is created by the changes we are willing to make."

Maxwell, John C. The 15 Invaluable Laws of Growth: Live Them and Reach Your Potential. Nashville: Center Street, 2012.

Maxwell, John C.

"People change when they hurt enough that they have to, learn enough that they want to, or receive enough that they are able to."

Maxwell, John C. Developing the Leader Within You. Nashville: Thomas Nelson, 1993.

Cialdini, Robert B.

Research on commitment and consistency referenced in Chapter 11.

Cialdini, Robert B. Influence: The Psychology of Persuasion. New York: William Morrow, 1984. Referenced in Maxwell, John C. in leadership and influence contexts.

Maxwell, John C.

"The secret of your success is found in your daily routine."

Maxwell, John C. Today Matters: 12 Daily Practices to Guarantee Tomorrow's Success. Nashville: Center Street, 2004.

Maxwell, John C.

“The greatest day in your life and mine is when we take total responsibility for our attitudes.”

Maxwell, John C. The Difference Maker: Making Your Attitude Your Greatest Asset. Nashville: Thomas Nelson, 2006.

Chapter 12 — Insurance and Financial Conversations

Maxwell, John C.

“A leader is someone who demonstrates what’s possible.”

Maxwell, John C. Leadership Gold: Lessons I’ve Learned from a Lifetime of Leading. Nashville: Thomas Nelson, 2008.

Maxwell, John C.

“The pessimist sees difficulty in every opportunity. The optimist sees the opportunity in every difficulty.”

Maxwell, John C. The Difference Maker: Making Your Attitude Your Greatest Asset. Nashville: Thomas Nelson, 2006.

Maxwell, John C.

“People don’t care how much you know until they know how much you care.”

Maxwell, John C. The 21 Irrefutable Laws of Leadership: Follow Them and People Will Follow You. Nashville: Thomas Nelson, 1998.

Carnegie, Dale.

Financial conversation partnership principle referenced in Chapter 12.

Carnegie, Dale. How to Win Friends and Influence People. New York: Simon and Schuster, 1936.

Chapter 13 — Treatment Acceptance and Clinical Communication

Maxwell, John C.

“If your actions inspire others to dream more, learn more, do more and become more, you are a leader.”

Maxwell, John C. The 21 Irrefutable Laws of Leadership: Follow Them and People Will Follow You. Nashville: Thomas Nelson, 1998.

Maxwell, John C.

“To add value to others, one must first value others.”

Maxwell, John C. Becoming a Person of Influence: How to Positively Impact the Lives of Others. Nashville: Thomas Nelson, 1997.

Maxwell, John C.

“Knowledge is power, but character is what gets things done.”

Maxwell, John C. The 21 Indispensable Qualities of a Leader: Becoming the Person Others Will Want to Follow. Nashville: Thomas Nelson, 1999.

Maxwell, John C.

"People don't care how much you know until they know how much you care."

Maxwell, John C. The 21 Irrefutable Laws of Leadership: Follow Them and People Will Follow You. Nashville: Thomas Nelson, 1998.

Carnegie, Dale.

"You can make more friends in two months by becoming interested in other people than you can in two years by trying to get other people interested in you."

Carnegie, Dale. How to Win Friends and Influence People. New York: Simon and Schuster, 1936.

Carnegie, Dale.

Patient motivation and influence principles referenced throughout Chapter 13.

Carnegie, Dale. How to Win Friends and Influence People. New York: Simon and Schuster, 1936.

Chapter 14 — Reactivation, Retention, and Team Leadership

Maxwell, John C.

"The secret to success is to do the common things uncommonly well."

Maxwell, John C. The Maxwell Daily Reader: 365 Days of Insight to Develop the Leader Within You and Influence Those Around You. Nashville: Thomas Nelson, 2007.

Carnegie, Dale.

"You can make more friends in two months by becoming interested in other people than you can in two years by trying to get other people interested in you."

Carnegie, Dale. How to Win Friends and Influence People. New York: Simon and Schuster, 1936. Cited in Maxwell, John C. leadership work.

Angelou, Maya.

"People will forget what you said. People will forget what you did. But people will never forget how you made them feel."

Angelou, Maya. Widely attributed in speeches and interviews throughout her career. Cited frequently in leadership literature including Maxwell, John C. Everyone Communicates, Few Connect. Nashville: Thomas Nelson, 2010.

Angelou, Maya.

"I've learned that whenever I decide something with an open heart, I usually make the right decision."

Angelou, Maya. Wouldn't Take Nothing for My Journey Now. New York: Random House, 1993.

Angelou, Maya.

"Try to be a rainbow in someone else's cloud."

Angelou, Maya. Letter to My Daughter. New York: Random House, 2008.

Maxwell, John C.

"Patience is not the ability to wait but the ability to keep a good attitude while waiting."

Maxwell, John C. The Difference Maker: Making Your Attitude Your Greatest Asset. Nashville: Thomas Nelson, 2006.

Maxwell, John C.

"The function of leadership is to produce more leaders, not more followers."

Maxwell, John C. The 21 Irrefutable Laws of Leadership: Follow Them and People Will Follow You. Nashville: Thomas Nelson, 1998.

Maxwell, John C.

"Great leaders are almost always great simplifiers, who can cut through argument, debate, and doubt to offer a solution everybody can understand and remember."

Maxwell, John C. Leadership Gold: Lessons I've Learned from a Lifetime of Leading. Nashville: Thomas Nelson, 2008.

Maxwell, John C.

"The quality of a leader is reflected in the standards they set for themselves."

Maxwell, John C. The 21 Indispensable Qualities of a Leader: Becoming the Person Others Will Want to Follow. Nashville: Thomas Nelson, 1999.

Chapter 15 — The Practice That A.L.I.G.N.s

Aristotle (attributed).

"Alone we can do so little; together we can do so much."

Commonly attributed to Aristotle in leadership literature. Cited in Maxwell, John C. The 17 Indisputable Laws of Teamwork. Nashville: Thomas Nelson, 2001. Note: This exact quote is sometimes attributed to Helen Keller; original Aristotle source unverified.

Maxwell, John C.

"The secret of your success is found in your daily routine."

Maxwell, John C. Today Matters: 12 Daily Practices to Guarantee Tomorrow's Success. Nashville: Center Street, 2004.

Sinek, Simon.

"People don't buy what you do; they buy why you do it."

Sinek, Simon. Start with Why: How Great Leaders Inspire Everyone to Take Action. New York: Portfolio/Penguin, 2009.

Brown, Brené.

"Connection is why we're here. It is what gives purpose and meaning to our lives."

Brown, Brené. The Gifts of Imperfection: Let Go of Who You Think You're Supposed to Be and Embrace Who You Are. Center City, MN: Hazelden Publishing, 2010.

Brown, Brené.

"Connection is the energy that exists between people when they feel seen, heard, and valued."

Brown, Brené. The Gifts of Imperfection: Let Go of Who You Think You're Supposed to Be and Embrace Who You Are. Center City, MN: Hazelden Publishing, 2010.

Brown, Brené.

"Daring to set boundaries is about having the courage to love ourselves, even when we risk disappointing others."

Brown, Brené. Daring Greatly: How the Courage to Be Vulnerable Transforms the Way We Live, Love, Parent, and Lead. New York: Gotham Books, 2012.

Chapter 16 — Your 90-Day A.L.I.G.N.™ Implementation Plan

Maxwell, John C.

"The beginning is the most important part of the work."

Maxwell, John C. The Maxwell Daily Reader: 365 Days of Insight to Develop the Leader Within You and Influence Those Around You. Nashville: Thomas Nelson, 2007. Note: This quote is also attributed to Plato in various sources; attribution in leadership literature is frequently to Maxwell's paraphrase.

Maxwell, John C.

"Success is not final, failure is not fatal: it is the courage to continue that counts."

Widely attributed to Winston Churchill in primary sources. Cited frequently by Maxwell, John C. in leadership development contexts. See Churchill, Winston S. Various speeches, 1940–1945. Public domain.

Maxwell, John C.

"To know thyself is the beginning of wisdom."

Attributed to Socrates in Plato's Dialogues, c. 380 BCE. Public domain. Cited in Maxwell, John C. leadership development contexts.

Conclusion — The Conversation That Changes Everything

Maxwell, John C.
"Leaders must be close enough to relate to others, but far enough ahead to motivate them."
Maxwell, John C. The 21 Irrefutable Laws of Leadership: Follow Them and People Will Follow You. Nashville: Thomas Nelson, 1998.

Maxwell, John C.

"The greatest gift you can give someone is the gift of your time and attention."

Maxwell, John C. Everyone Communicates, Few Connect: What the Most Effective People Do Differently. Nashville: Thomas Nelson, 2010.

Master Bibliography

All sources cited in Four Minutes and Seventeen Seconds: How One Conversation Changes Everything in a Dental Practice, listed alphabetically by author.

Angelou, Maya.

Letter to My Daughter.

New York: Random House, 2008.

Angelou, Maya.

Wouldn't Take Nothing for My Journey Now.

New York: Random House, 1993.

Aristotle.

Metaphysica (Metaphysics).

c. 350 BCE. Public domain. Multiple modern translations available.

Aristotle.

Nicomachean Ethics.

c. 350 BCE. Public domain. Multiple modern translations available.

Brown, Brené.

Daring Greatly: How the Courage to Be Vulnerable Transforms the Way We Live, Love, Parent, and Lead.

New York: Gotham Books, 2012.

Brown, Brené.

The Gifts of Imperfection: Let Go of Who You Think You're Supposed to Be and Embrace Who You Are.

Center City, MN: Hazelden Publishing, 2010.

Carnegie, Dale.

How to Win Friends and Influence People.

New York: Simon and Schuster, 1936.

Cialdini, Robert B.

Influence: The Psychology of Persuasion.

New York: William Morrow, 1984.

Churchill, Winston S.

Various speeches and writings, 1940–1945. Public domain.

Durant, Will.

The Story of Philosophy: The Lives and Opinions of the World's Greatest Philosophers.

New York: Simon and Schuster, 1926.
Maxwell, John C.

Becoming a Person of Influence: How to Positively Impact the Lives of Others.

Nashville: Thomas Nelson, 1997.
Maxwell, John C.

Developing the Leader Within You.

Nashville: Thomas Nelson, 1993.
Maxwell, John C.

The Difference Maker: Making Your Attitude Your Greatest Asset.

Nashville: Thomas Nelson, 2006.
Maxwell, John C.

Everyone Communicates, Few Connect: What the Most Effective People Do Differently.

Nashville: Thomas Nelson, 2010.
Maxwell, John C.

Failing Forward: Turning Mistakes into Stepping Stones for Success.

Nashville: Thomas Nelson, 2000.
Maxwell, John C.

Intentional Living: Choosing a Life That Matters.

Nashville: Center Street, 2015.
Maxwell, John C.

Leadership Gold: Lessons I've Learned from a Lifetime of Leading.

Nashville: Thomas Nelson, 2008.
Maxwell, John C.

The 15 Invaluable Laws of Growth: Live Them and Reach Your Potential.

Nashville: Center Street, 2012.
Maxwell, John C.

The Maxwell Daily Reader: 365 Days of Insight to Develop the Leader Within You and Influence Those Around You.

Nashville: Thomas Nelson, 2007.
Maxwell, John C.

Put Your Dream to the Test: 10 Questions to Help You See It and Seize It.

Nashville: Thomas Nelson, 2009.
Maxwell, John C.

The 17 Indisputable Laws of Teamwork: Embrace Them and Empower Your Team.

Nashville: Thomas Nelson, 2001.
Maxwell, John C.

The 21 Indispensable Qualities of a Leader: Becoming the Person Others Will Want to Follow.

Nashville: Thomas Nelson, 1999.
Maxwell, John C.

The 21 Irrefutable Laws of Leadership: Follow Them and People Will Follow You.

Nashville: Thomas Nelson, 1998.
Maxwell, John C.

The 360 Degree Leader: Developing Your Influence from Anywhere in the Organization.

Nashville: Thomas Nelson, 2005.
Maxwell, John C.

Today Matters: 12 Daily Practices to Guarantee Tomorrow's Success.

Nashville: Center Street, 2004.
Robbins, Anthony.

Awaken the Giant Within: How to Take Immediate Control of Your Mental, Emotional, Physical and Financial Destiny.

New York: Free Press, 1991.
Shaw, George Bernard (attributed).
"The single biggest problem in communication is the illusion that it has taken place." Widely attributed. Original source in Shaw's published works unverified. Cited in Maxwell, John C. Everyone Communicates, Few Connect. Nashville: Thomas Nelson, 2010.
Sinek, Simon.

Start with Why: How Great Leaders Inspire Everyone to Take Action.

New York: Portfolio/Penguin, 2009.

Notes on Attribution

John Maxwell Quotes

John Maxwell is a prolific author whose ideas have been expressed across dozens of books, speeches, and leadership development programs over more than four decades. Several quotes attributed to Maxwell throughout this book appear in multiple sources within his body of work and have been attributed to the most commonly cited primary source. Readers seeking the original context of any Maxwell quote are encouraged to consult the complete Maxwell bibliography at www.johnmaxwell.com.

George Bernard Shaw Attribution

The quote "The single biggest problem in communication is the illusion that it has taken place" is widely attributed to George Bernard Shaw in leadership literature but has not been definitively traced to a specific Shaw publication. It is possible this quote originated with or was significantly popularized by its use in leadership development contexts. It is cited here as it appears most commonly in the literature.

Aristotle Paraphrases

The quote "We are what we repeatedly do. Excellence, then, is not an act, but a habit" is frequently attributed directly to Aristotle but is actually a paraphrase by Will Durant from The Story of Philosophy (1926), summarizing Aristotle's argument in Nicomachean Ethics. The sentiment is authentically Aristotelian though the exact wording is Durant's.

Maya Angelou Quotes

The quote "People will forget what you said. People will forget what you did. But people will never forget how you made them feel" is widely attributed to Maya Angelou and was used with her implicit endorsement throughout her public life, though it has also been attributed to Carl W. Buehner. Angelou's endorsement of the sentiment through decades of public attribution makes her the most appropriate citation in a leadership context.

Public Domain Sources

Quotes attributed to Abraham Lincoln, Theodore Roosevelt, Winston Churchill, Aristotle, and George Bernard Shaw are from public domain sources. These authors' works are no longer protected by copyright in the United States.

For questions about specific citations or to report a citation error, contact Practice Management Systems® at david@practice-sys.com.

Practice Management Systems®
Oregon City, Oregon
www.practice-sys.com

Made in the USA
Las Vegas, NV
29 June 2026

50113415R00134